Living at a Higher Level of Faith

Living at a Higher Level of Faith

Calvin Rychener

NORTHWOODS
COMMUNITY CHURCH

PEORIA, ILLINOIS 61615 USA

We want to hear from you.
Please send your comments about this book
to us in care of the address below. Thank you.

Calvin Rychener
Northwoods Community Church
10700 N. Allen Rd.
Peoria, IL 61615

To My Lord Jesus Christ
Who called me to Faith

To my father and mother, Lloyd and Marie Rychener,
Who brought me up in the Faith

To my beautiful wife, Susan,
Who journeys with me in Faith

To my children, Kathryn, Jonathon, Victoria and Nathan
Who will carry on the Faith

TABLE OF CONTENTS

ACKNOWLEDGMENTS

I'd like to say thank you:

To Susan Rychener, who has always encouraged me to write;

To Dave Pfanschmidt, without whose help this book would not have happened;

To Sherie Hittinger, my administrative assistant who makes life much easier for me;

To the staff at Northwoods Community Church, for allowing me the wonderful privilege of leading them and partnering together with them on an incredible journey of faith;

To my faithful prayer partners who provide the wind beneath my wings;

To the congregation of Northwoods Community Church for enduring thirteen years of my pastoring;

To the elders and board members who have been incredible "faith partners" in this ministry;

To several cheerleaders, Jay, Evelyn, and Dawn to name a few, who about the time I'd be ready to give up the idea would say, "When are you going to write your book?" (I've always known with you in my corner, I'd sell at least three copies!);

And to the many people in my past who have been a part of my faith journey including:

The congregation of Archbold Evangelical Mennonite Church, in Archbold, OH, who nurtured my faith for the first eighteen years of my life (Go Streaks!); and

The congregation of Grabill Church in Grabill, IN, with whom I cut my teeth in pastoral ministry.

PREFACE

To me, it seems only appropriate that my long-held dream of writing a book should find its initial expression with this book, *Living at a Higher Level of Faith*. The journey to this book has itself, been a journey of faith.

God first planted within me the seed and desire to write when I attended a workshop at a Billy Graham Crusade in April of 1987. The appeal I heard from the seminar leader that day was, "Why aren't more of you pastors publishing your material?"

Of course, the thought to me at that point seemed a bit presumptuous. *Who am I to write a book? I'm not big enough, bright enough, eloquent enough, nor do I have anything to say that would be worth reading.* You can tell, I've always had an abundance of self confidence.

In the ensuing years since that first seed in 1987 to now, God has done a lot of internal healing within me, apart from which, this book would not be a reality. (In fact, God willing, my next book will deal with issues of internal healing). But, that journey to healing itself has been a journey of faith. Along the way I have been helped by many different Christian authors and teachers, most notably, David Seamonds, whose book, *Healing of Memories*, first started me on the journey, and John Maxwell, whose weekly tapes and many books have helped me rise to a higher level of faith.

Having decided in 1996 that I was going to write a book some day, the question became, where do you start and how do you get started? Lingering questions about who would read what I have to say still plagued me at times. I jokingly say, "God dealt with that issue one night when I walked into Barnes & Noble and noticed that there were thousands of authors who had nothing to say, but who apparently hadn't let that stop them from writing."

Finally, after trying to make a number of initial runs at it on my own, one night in the summer of 2001, I prayed in desperation, "God, if this is your idea and you really want me to publish a book, you're going to have to bring someone to me who can help me, because I can't do this on my own and I don't want it to occupy my mind if it's not going to happen."

Would you believe that the very next night, God in His sovereign way, linked me up with the man who is most responsible for this book you now hold in your hands? God sent Dave Pfanschmidt to me as a direct answer to prayer and he has carried the torch for getting this book into print from that day until now.

The individual chapters that appear in this book were first preached as messages at Northwoods Community Church, the church I pastor in Peoria, IL. With Dave's help, these messages have been modified and transcribed from the spoken word to print and thus, hopefully will make for interesting and easy reading. As well, as will be readily apparent, these messages were written not for the ivory tower theologian, but for the common person who is simply seeking to flesh out his/her faith in Christ in our every day world.

Now that this book is a reality, I pray that God will bless the lives of all who read it and that they truly will live at a higher level of faith. When I consider that the Bible says in Hebrews 11:6, "Without faith it is impossible to please God," I can't imagine a more important quality to develop in our lives.

Someone once said, "Enthusiasm is nothing but faith with a tin can tied to its tail." While my tin can may not be loud, it is yet real. Therefore, to the degree that my can, through this book, arouses "enthusiastic faith" in someone else, I give all the glory to Jesus, "the author and perfecter of our faith."

CHAPTER ONE

*"Faith is being sure of what we hope for
and certain of what we do not see."*

HEBREWS 11:1

UNDERSTANDING THE IMPORTANCE OF FAITH

During the summer of 2000, my daughter, Kathryn, who was 14-years-old at the time, attended a week of camp at Miracle Camp in Lawton, MI. Upon her return home, we were excited to learn about the events of the week, friends she had made, her counselor and other girls who had been in her cabin. During our discussion, Kathryn showed me pictures of some of the new friends she had met at camp. One of her favorites was a photo of a girl named Julie Short, who had been in her cabin.

All of a sudden, a rush of memories came back to me regarding that name. I asked her, "Kathryn, do you know if Julie lives in the Fort Wayne area and if her mom and dad are Doug and Joanne Short?"

Kathryn said, "Yes, that's her!"

I said, "Kates, you're not going to believe this, but you and Julie occupied cribs in the same nursery at my first church. You used to roll around the nursery floor together. She was one of your first friends. And not only that, but Julie was a miracle baby in that church." And then I went on to recount a story that had lain dormant in my memory for many years.

A few days after Julie was born, we received word from her parents that she was experiencing some difficulties and was being taken to the hospital for tests. In a very rapid sequence of events, Julie was transported from Fort Wayne to Indianapolis. She was diagnosed as having a very rare and deadly serious complication with her liver, which in turn was placing considerable stress on her heart. In fact, her heart was twice the size that it was supposed to be and she was experiencing congestive heart failure.

On Saturday night, just one week after she was born, the doctors in Indianapolis informed Doug and Joanne that if the grandparents wanted to see their granddaughter alive, they needed to come to the hospital that night. Julie was not expected to make it until the next morning. Thus it was that I received a call late at night from the grandfather, who was a member of my church. Through tears, he informed me, "Cal, they've called us down to Indianapolis. They don't expect Julie to live through the night, so we're going now." I assured him that we would be in prayer, that they should call if anything happened and that I would inform the congregation in the morning.

IT WAS AS IF I KNEW THAT GOD WANTED US, AS A CHURCH, TO SEEK HIM FOR JULIE'S LIFE

As I hung up, my heart was just sick. I imagined what it would be like were it the life of my own newborn hanging in the balance. I prayed. I asked God, even at this late hour, to reverse the situation and give us a miracle. Then I went to bed, fully expecting to get a phone call sometime during the night.

By morning, I had heard nothing. As I spent some quiet time with God, I sensed that He had quickened some verses on faith to my spirit, verses like Matthew 9:29, which says, "According to your faith will it be done to you." Or John 14:14, "You may ask me for anything in my name and I will do it." And it was as if I knew that God wanted us, as a church, to seek Him for Julie's life.

My expectation that God might grant us a wonderful miracle began to grow as His Word came alive in my heart.

As the worship service was about to begin that morning, I remember walking out on the platform and being met by a palpable sense of heaviness hanging over the congregation of 150 people. This was making it virtually impossible to enter into worship with any sense of joy, hope or faith in God's presence. So on this morning, I started the service differently than I had ever done before or have done since.

I simply stepped to the microphone and said to the people gathered there that day, "Folks, I just sense that we are all very sad and have brought heavy hearts to the service today because of what is happening in little Julie's life." I told them what the grandfather had said the night before and that if there was any good news to focus on this morning, it was the fact that Julie had apparently made it through the night when she wasn't expected to.

I told them about the faith promises that I felt the Spirit had spoken to my heart that morning and that even now I sensed God was calling us to seek Him by faith. "So," I said, "I want to begin this morning with all of us, in groups of three and four, taking time to pray that God will spare Julie's life and heal her." And then, for the next several minutes, that small church came alive with a buzz of people praying as we lifted Julie, and her mom and dad, before God's throne in heaven. After a few minutes, I closed in prayer and then we began to sing with a markedly different sense of hope than what we had brought into the service a few minutes earlier.

But none of us could have been prepared for what happened next. Not more than five minutes later, during the reading of the

FOR THE NEXT SEVERAL MINUTES, THAT SMALL CHURCH CAME ALIVE WITH A BUZZ OF PEOPLE PRAYING

Scriptures, a phone rang in the office area. Since the offices were right next to the sanctuary of our small church, everybody could hear it ringing. My associate pastor slipped out quickly to answer it and, within about two minutes, came back in and handed me a slip of paper. The note read, "Cal, the call was from Doug and Joanne. Just moments ago, the head of pediatrics was called in. He has seen a case similar to this and is hopeful that a procedure he has outlined will save Julie's life. They've upgraded her chances of survival from zero to 50-50!"

When I stepped up to the pulpit to share that news, not less than 10 minutes after the entire church had been in prayer, there was an audible gasp from the congregation. God could not have made it more clear to us that day that He was working in answer to our prayers than if He had dropped a note from heaven saying: "I have heard you and am responding to your prayers." In fact, people would tell me for several years after that, "I will never forget that service. That was unbelievable."

THERE, IN THAT ROOM AND ON THAT NIGHT, WE CALLED ON GOD AGAIN

Now let me tell you the rest of the story. Just getting some hope that Julie might survive for a while was one thing. But the hope of Julie becoming healthy was an all-together different matter. In fact, the doctors set a goal of getting her to six months and 10 pounds, whereupon she could be placed on a list for a liver transplant. But that was not what we were asking God for. We were asking Him for a complete healing, something that none of the specialists at that time held out any hope for. Julie made it through those first couple of days. Though her situation began to stabilize, she remained very, very sick, as the fundamental problem remained.

Shortly thereafter, my wife, Susan, and I, along with our associate pastor and his wife, made the two-hour trip to

Indianapolis where we had the chance to pray for Julie. She was hooked up to all kinds of tubes and was very sickly. She lay in one of those small, covered, tent-like incubators and we could only touch her by inserting our hands into a pair of rubber gloves that were attached to the side of the incubator. She was to have no human contact other than being touched by those rubber gloves.

I reached into that incubator and gently laid my hands on her fragile little body. There, in that room and on that night, we called on God again and said, "Lord, as you have shown us mercy and answered our prayers thus far, we're asking you for a complete healing on Julie's behalf. Please drive this disease from her body, restore function to her organs, and let her live to praise your name, Oh God!"

Incredibly, within one week, Julie was out of the intensive care unit. Two weeks later, she was on her way home from the hospital. For the first month, Doug and Joanne made weekly trips to Indianapolis so that her condition could be closely monitored. For the first year, they made monthly trips. And each time, they would come home encouraged that Julie was getting better, though it seemed that the complications with the liver remained. Over time, the predictions regarding her chances of survival were gradually upgraded. But the dire prognosis remained: without a liver transplant she could not live beyond five to seven years.

Finally, after the first year, the parents were told that they only needed to come back every six months for a check-up. So, six months later they returned to the hospital for their bi-annual checkup and returned home with a miraculous report.

The doctor, after taking some updated tests, came into the room with a very puzzled look on his face. He said to Doug and Joanne, "If I didn't know better, I wouldn't believe that the test results I'm holding here belong to Julie. But I know they're hers and I know these are her files. I have absolutely no explanation for the results that I am looking at right now. According to these tests, your daughter is as healthy and whole as any other normal child her age. There is no trace of the former condition in her system, her organs are fully functional, and there's no reason she shouldn't live to be 90."

"In fact," he continued, "there really is no reason why you should have to come back here. It's unexplainable, but Julie is completely well!" And 14 years later, my daughter was showing me pictures of Julie - the little girl that God had used to teach us that He still does mighty works in response to the cry of faith!

The longer I live and walk with Jesus Christ, the more I am coming to understand the vital importance of faith. Not only is it the critical element to receiving the mighty works God wants to release to us, but also to living the kind of life God designed us to live.

If you're not getting the rewards that God wants to give you by faith, you're getting ripped off

The Vital Importance of Faith

How important is faith? Well, it might surprise you to learn that the Bible says there's only one way to gain God's approval. It's not by being more good than bad. It's not by keeping the Ten Commandments. It's not by trying to be a better person. It's not by trying to be religious and going to church! Rather, the Bible says in Hebrews 11:6, "Without faith, it's impossible to please God." That's pretty amazing, isn't it? In fact, just so you don't miss it, read this next sentence very carefully.

Faith is the only way to get God's approval! There's only one way to get His smile on your life and that is by living a life of faith in His Son, Jesus Christ! When you just think of that statement, "Without faith, it's impossible to please God," that makes faith pretty important, wouldn't you say?

In fact, that verse goes on to say that if you have faith, it reveals two basic beliefs in your life. The first is that you believe God exists and therefore you go to Him with the problems and challenges and needs of your life. If you don't believe God exists, you handle them on your own. Secondly, if you have faith, you believe God rewards those who earnestly seek Him. People who truly have faith in God believe that in coming to Him with their problems and perplexities, something different will happen than if they just tried to work it out on their own. They believe that God rewards them for coming to Him in faith. Yes, faith is the only way to get God's approval. But there's more!

Faith is the only way to get God's rewards! If you're not getting the rewards that God wants to give you by faith, you're getting ripped off.

Jim Cymbala says in his book, *Fresh Faith*, "We see now why the great target of Satan is to break down our faith. He knows that faith is our lifeline to God, so he aims at cutting that lifeline. Faith is like the hand that reaches up to receive what God has freely promised. If our enemy can pull your hand back down to your side, then he has succeeded. All of God's intended supply will just stay where it is in heaven."[1] When that happens, you're getting ripped off!

I recently cut a very unusual story out of the newspaper about a lady named Mary Hutton, who died in April of 2001 at the age of 95. She was a bit of a curiosity in that she slept in the hallway of her boarding house so each room could have a tenant. The *Courier-Journal* of Louisville reported, "She lived in a little cubicle in the hallway with a sheet around her so she wouldn't take up one of the bedrooms."

The ironic thing is that when she died, Mary left $3.5 million to her alma mater, Western Kentucky University. Ron Beck, the university's former director of planned giving said, "She saved money because she never thought she had enough to live on. She was a multi-millionaire who didn't realize the value of her savings."[2]

That's what I call getting ripped off! Imagine living as a pauper when all the time she could have been living at a higher level were it not for the fact that her eyes had been blinded to her true wealth. The sad fact is that this happens all the time in the spiritual realm when we fail to appropriate by faith what God wants to give us through His promises.

And to be sure, God has given us a wealth of incredible promises. The apostle Peter says in 2 Peter 1:3-4, "By His mighty power, God has given us all the rich and wonderful blessings He promised." But, the only way we receive the benefits of those promises in our lives is to appropriate them by faith.

WE ALL UNDERSTAND FAITH BECAUSE EACH OF US EXERCISES NATURAL-LEVEL FAITH EVERY DAY

For instance, God has said, "Whosoever believes in my Son, Jesus Christ, will have his sins forgiven and will be given eternal life."[3] That's a promise, but the only way that promise is activated in your life is through faith whereby you say, "Okay, I'm going to trust Jesus Christ for my forgiveness and salvation. I'm staking my life on what He's said and I will follow Him."

If we don't exercise faith in God's promises, we will miss out on the rewards that He would otherwise give us! And my hope is that through this book, your faith will grow and you will truly live at a higher level, enjoying God's approval and rewards in your life while at the same time, not allowing the devil to rip you off concerning those things God wants to give you. Faith is so important! It literally is the key that unlocks the door to heaven's provisions in your life. Because faith is so important, it's critical that we understand:

The Vital Aspects of Higher-Level Faith

Just what is faith and how easy or difficult is it to exercise faith? It might help us to distinguish between two types of faith, Natural-Level Faith and Higher-Level Faith, to demonstrate the fact that we all live by faith to some extent every day.

Natural-Level Faith is simply acting in accordance with your sensory-based beliefs. In this regard, everyone exercises faith all the time. Every time you do anything, your actions are based upon a belief that is informed by your senses. When you are driving your car and need to slow down or stop, you step on the brake (*action*) because of your intuitive sense (*belief*) that the car will stop when you apply pressure on the brake. You have no proof in advance that your car will stop, but your sensory experience from having stepped on the brake thousands of times before tells you that it will.   That's natural-level faith.

YOU CANNOT DIVORCE TRUE FAITH FROM HOW YOU LIVE YOUR LIFE

Whenever you sit down in a chair, do you examine it first or run a test to see how much pressure per square inch the seat will hold before you sit down? No! You sit down (*action*) based upon your intuitive sense (*belief*) that the seat will hold you. You don't know with certainty, before you sit down, that the seat will hold you. But nonetheless, you take the chance that it will, without a second thought, because of what your subconscious sensory experience has taught you about the ability of chairs to support you. Again, that's natural-level faith. Such faith is absolutely essential to a normal and healthy functioning in our every day world.   In this sense, we all understand faith because each of us exercises natural-level faith every day.

But, when it comes to the kind of faith that pleases God, we're talking about a **Higher-Level Faith** that transcends the natural realm and our five senses. This is the kind of faith that is referred to in Hebrews 11:6, without which we cannot please God. Natural-level faith has nothing to do with pleasing God. A person can exercise that kind of faith every day of his life and never have cause to think of God. But higher-level faith begins and ends in a relationship with God.

We might define this kind of faith as *"living with the positive expectation that God will fulfill His promises, even before He does!"* There are a number of vital aspects to this definition that we need to grab hold of. The first involves the word "living."

POSITIVE THINKING

NEEDS TO BE

GROUNDED

IN REALITY

Faith that pleases God impacts our living. In other words, it's much more than mere mental assent to a religious creed. While a creed can often summarize various tenants of "the faith," the truth is that Satan has a very accurate creed concerning who Jesus Christ is. Satan knows that Jesus Christ died and rose again and has been given all authority in heaven and earth. Satan knows that Jesus will, one day, doom him and his angels to hell!

The important phrase here is *living and acting based upon that creed.* You cannot divorce true faith from how you live your life. If you have faith in who Jesus Christ says He is and what He did for you, than you live like it! You don't just passively assent to it.

Then too, *higher-level faith, of necessity, includes expectation,* because we're waiting on God to fulfill what He hasn't yet! Hebrews 11:1 says, "Now faith is being sure of what we hope for and certain of what we do not see!" The fact that I'm "hoping for something" indicates that I haven't yet received it in its material form. And because it hasn't materialized yet, I can't visibly prove to anyone else that which I'm so certain of. It's something like an expectant mother who may be only a few weeks along. She says, "I'm going to have a baby," even though there is, as of yet, no proof to the natural eye that she is pregnant. Yet, long before anyone else can see it, she's certain of what she does not yet see. And nine months later, the promise of that child comes to fruition for all to see.

Notice as well, *higher-level faith is inherently positive!* That doesn't mean we may not get discouraged sometimes while we're waiting for God to fulfill a promise. But faith is hope-filled expectation concerning the future based upon God's promises. As such, it's much more than mere positive thinking. While faith should always lead to positive thinking, the vital difference with faith is that it is positive thinking based upon God's truth, not just upon something I want to be true.

ONLY GOD'S RELEASING HIS ANSWERS IN TIME AND SPACE VERIFIES WHAT FAITH HAS SEEN AND SPOKEN BEFOREHAND

Some proponents of positive thinking speak, at times, as if just being positive about something long enough will make it happen. I can be positive all I want about my prospects for flooring Mike Tyson in the boxing ring, but I'm fairly sure that all my positive thinking wouldn't change the results of such a match. Positive thinking needs to be grounded in reality, not in the denial of reality.

I love the story of the little boy who came home from school and said, "Dad, I think I flunked my math test." His dad said, "Come on son, you need to think and speak a little more positively than that." Whereupon the boy said, "Okay, I'm positive I flunked my math test." Faith is inherently positive and leads to positive thinking, but it is much more than trying to change reality or deny reality by thinking positively.

Next, *higher-level faith has as its object God's character and God's Word.* As such, faith receives God's smile because it, in essence, says, "God, I believe you! I believe you are there and that you are in control even though I can't see you! And I believe that you will do what you have promised, even when I can't make sense out of what is going on!"

One young child defined faith as "believing what you know isn't true." Though humorous, it's a definition that is fatally wrong. Faith is "believing what you know is true, though God hasn't yet verified it in time!" As such, I can't prove to you that God will keep His promise, until He does so. Which means as well that:

Higher-level faith engages us in tension. I'm living, believing, acting and speaking as if I have already received what is not yet here. For instance, I know I have received salvation today. I know that heaven is my future home, but I don't have it materially yet and thus I can't prove it to you. Sometimes, as in Julie Short's case, God may quicken His Word to our hearts. Perhaps He wants us to believe Him for healing or a specific answer to prayer. This engages us in a tension because when God implants a promise in our heart for some specific situation, we're then pregnant with the knowledge of what God is going to do. But if we say something about it before it materializes, we have to be prepared to look foolish to everyone else because we have no proof of what we do not yet possess materially. We have the substance of the thing hoped for, but we don't yet have the actual thing.

For example, there was a day when I parked my car alongside the road that ran next to the 40 acres of land upon which we one day hoped to build our church. I prayed by faith that God would allow us to reach hundreds of people for Jesus Christ, thus necessitating a facility that would seat several thousand. I envisioned that building in my mind's eye before it came to be and while our attendance was less than 500 people. What seemed foolish at that time is now reality today. Only God's releasing His answers in time and space verifies what faith has seen and spoken beforehand.

But what He has spoken He will verify because *higher-level faith originates with God.* In other words, it's important for us to understand that faith is not figuring out something we want and then trying to use God to get it. No, true faith comes from God as we receive His living Word into our hearts. Then a supernatural music comes alive within us as the product of that faith. God speaks and, as I receive it in my heart, faith is borne![4]

I'm convinced today that if all of us could experience even a little taste of some of God's rewards that come by faith, we'd be doing everything we could to develop our faith in order to live at a higher level. Wherever you are in your own faith walk, even if you haven't yet stepped across the line of faith, I hope this book will release expectation in your life for what God wants to do to take you to a higher level of living. Will you open your heart to that possibility right now?

> *Lord, I open my heart to all that you want to teach me about living at a higher level of faith. I believe that you exist and that you reward those who earnestly seek you. Therefore, I set my heart on seeking you. Develop within me a faith that is pleasing to you and a faith that can receive all that you want to release to me. In Jesus name, Amen.*

Now let's take a look at the exciting possibilities faith can release in our lives.

CHAPTER TWO

*"Therefore I tell you, whatever you ask for in prayer,
believe that you have received it, and it will be yours."*

MARK 11:24

RELEASING FAITH'S POTENTIAL

I recently read a great story about a man who learned a rather unpleasant lesson when his attempt to steal some gasoline went awry. He was apparently trying to siphon the gasoline from a motor home parked on a side street in Seattle. Anyone who has ever attempted to siphon gasoline from a tank knows that there is always a danger that you might get a mouthful. Well, this was our hero's lucky day.

Police arrived at the scene to find a man curled up next to the motor home as sick as could be. A police spokesman said the man admitted trying to steal gasoline, but he got the surprise of his life when he inadvertently plugged his hose into the motor home's sewage tank instead and then took a hit of that stuff. That's what you call getting a whole lot less than you bargained for . . . a wasted opportunity. That's having your expectations abruptly altered. The owner of the vehicle declined to press charges, saying it was the best laugh he'd ever had.

Getting less than one bargained for while attempting to siphon gasoline is one thing, but it's an all together different story when we get less than we bargained for on our faith journey. Perhaps you have known a time in your life when you desperately needed God to respond to your cries of faith. Even though you legitimately hooked the hose of your faith and prayer into the vast storage tank of God's promises, you got a whole lot less than you bargained for! And it has left you heart sick.

Perhaps you were crying out for the healing of a loved one, and he or she died anyway. You might have been crying out for a breakthrough with your child, and things only got worse. Maybe you cried out for your marriage to be saved, and it ended anyway. You asked God specifically for that job you needed, and somebody else got it. And once your faith has been dashed by disappointment and your expectations crushed, you say things like, "Well, that's the last time I'm going to let myself hope for something," because dashed expectations always leave you with a very bad taste in your mouth.

DASHED EXPECTATIONS ALWAYS LEAVE YOU WITH A VERY BAD TASTE IN YOUR MOUTH

I've been there myself. No two people could have been more disappointed than Susan and I were back in 1989, where we witnessed God's moving in answer to our prayers for the saving of our little child's life. We prayed from Week 10, when we were told we were going to lose the child, all the way out to Week 25, at which point it looked like every specific issue we had prayed about had worked out. The doctors were surprised and we were bragging about God's goodness and power. And then came Week 26 when Christopher was born three months prematurely. Even at that point, we couldn't imagine that God had brought us this far for things not to work out. But 10 hours later, Christopher died! And I felt like I had gotten a whole lot less than I had bargained for.

Only, unlike the unlucky gasoline robber, I wasn't attempting to steal anything from God. I was only doing what He had told me to do and that was to drink in His promises through faith. And, in the aftermath, I learned my lesson: I didn't know if I could ever trust God again. I felt like if faith in Him doesn't work when you most need it, then what good is it? It's an issue we need to come to grips with because sooner or later in our faith journey, every one of us will experience disappointment and dashed expectations. Thus, I want to help you gain the things promised by God to those who walk in true faith, while at the same time alerting you to the dangers of presumption that can give you a lot less than you bargained for.

One of the greatest statements on faith in the Bible is found in Mark 11:23-24. Jesus said, "I tell you the truth, if anyone says to this mountain, 'Go, throw yourself into the sea,' and does not doubt in his heart but believes that what he says will happen, it will be done for him. Therefore I tell you, whatever you ask for in prayer, believe that you have received it, and it will be yours." This is an incredible statement about the mountain-moving potential of faith. But it's also a dangerous statement in that it can be easily misapplied, to our own detriment, and has been many times by well-meaning but over-zealous people.

> WHEN WE'VE PRAYED
> FOR SOMETHING,
> WE'VE GOT TO
> BELIEVE IT BEFORE
> WE RECEIVE IT

Sometimes people treat a tremendous promise like this as if it's the only statement on faith in the Bible. Rather than placing these verses alongside all the other faith teaching in the Bible, they use a passage like this to treat God as if He's some kind of heavenly slot machine. I've actually heard a person say, "God has to do what I tell Him to, because He has set up the laws of faith and He is bound by those laws. So when I use my faith and say something is supposed to happen, it has to happen!" And on the surface, let's admit that these two verses do swing some control over to us. In other words, we've got to tell the mountain to move before it moves. When we've prayed for something, we've got to believe it before we receive it.

But what these verses don't say, that provide a balancing perspective with the rest of the Bible's teaching on faith, is that God must put into my heart what it is He wants me to believe before I can speak it and have it happen. Otherwise, my speaking and believing is mere wishful thinking. For example, in Genesis 18:10, God told 99-year-old Abraham and his 89-year-old wife who had been barren all her life, that they would have a child the next year. Yeah, right! But, you see, only because he had received that promise from God, could Abraham speak and act with the assurance that it was going to take place. He wasn't acting on some crazy notion that originated within his own mind.

> I CAN'T BE SURE WHETHER MY DESIRE IS JUST SOMETHING I WANT OR IF IT'S SOMETHING GOD HAS PUT ON MY HEART TO TRUST HIM FOR

It wasn't as if he was sitting in his rocker one day when the thought occurred to him, "You know, I've always wanted a child so I'm going to just start believing for one, even though I'm 99." At that point, he would have been off his rocker! That would have been presumption. But since God had placed the promise into his heart, Abraham didn't have to worry about the mountain-sized obstacles of old age and infertility because he knew God had made the promise. He had the witness in his heart! And Max Lucado brilliantly captures the absurdity of it all when he writes that a year later Sarah was the first lady in town to "pay her pediatrician with a Social Security check."[1]

Sometimes I have a strong desire in my heart for something to take place and I really want to be sure I'm walking in faith and speaking to that mountain by faith. But I can't be sure whether my desire is just something I want or if it's something God has put on my heart to trust Him for. What do I do in that situation to be sure that I'm not walking in presumption and setting myself up for disappointment if my prayer goes unanswered? It's helped me to understand that God's promises fall into various categories and my faith can be only as strong as the category warrants.

The first category of promises refers to those that are mine positionally, positively and experientially upon my trusting God by faith because of His specific promise to give these gifts to those who ask. This category includes the forgiveness of my sins, eternal life and the assurance that heaven is my home, a new heart, help in temptation and the Holy Spirit's indwelling power and presence.

If I've put my faith in Jesus Christ, I can know with absolute assurance that these promises have already been fulfilled in my life because of my position in Christ and that I'm already experiencing their realities in my life. These promises come to us immediately upon our placing our faith in Christ and we can have complete trust in them with no fear of disappointment.

GOD WANTS US TO TRUST HIM IF WHAT WE RECEIVE IS DIFFERENT FROM WHAT WE ASKED FOR

A second category of promises refers to those that are mine positionally and positively, but not yet experientially because they await a future fulfillment. This category includes that moment in heaven when I will be given a new body. There will be no more mourning or crying or pain or death. I won't grow old. I'll be perfect and will never have to admit to my wife or kids again, "I was wrong." (Won't that be fun)! Now, these promises too are mine by faith today due to my position in Christ, and they were guaranteed to me when I trusted Jesus as my Savior. But I will not experience them first-hand until later . . . unless I happen to get that "perfection" one down a little early!

But then there is a third category of promises that gives rise to some of our greatest faith conundrums. *These promises are mine potentially, but not positively, and only experientially if God grants them upon the release of my faith.* They are potential because of some other factors in God's divine wisdom and will, beyond my position in Christ and the mere expression of my faith, that determine whether or not I receive them.

I personally put physical healing in this category along with financial blessing, protection from hardship and struggle, the healing of a marriage, etc. God has made many general promises with regards to these issues. But in each specific instance, when I need Him to answer my prayers regarding these types of issues, I must seek Him for what He desires to do. While He will always respond to my faith, I am not personally guaranteed that I will always get what I specifically asked for. God may say "yes", "no", or "not yet" in response to my faith when it's a potential gift, but not one that is positively guaranteed. For instance, if He always guaranteed healing every time we asked, no one would ever die. But at the same time, I want to make sure I live as long as I can and as healthily as I can because I seek God for His healing in my life when I need it!

Please understand, God permits a bit of push back from us here. This faith walk He invites us on is a living and dynamic enterprise. In Isaiah 38:1-8, King Hezekiah was sick and at the point of death and was told by the prophet Isaiah to get his house in order because he would not recover. At which point, Hezekiah prayed to the Lord and wept bitterly that God would allow him to live longer. And amazingly God said, "I have heard your prayers and seen your tears so I am going to add 15 years to your life." Apparently God allows some flexibility for our faith here.

So we don't want to take a fatalistic approach in this category and say, "Whatever will be will be! Our faith doesn't affect what God does." That's not true. God wants us to seek Him for what we need and desire, but to trust Him if what we receive is different from what we asked for. At the same time, we want to make sure that a failure to receive an answer in this category doesn't cause us to lose sight of what we are assured in categories one and two, because those are the promises to which we have anchored our future hope, regardless of what happens in this life! We must not anchor our faith to the potential fulfillment of a promise the same way we do to a positional one.

Now, all of that said, the common factor in each category of promise is that they are all accessed by faith. Faith is the only way that we receive anything from God. Faith has the potential to release to us all of God's greatest resources in time and eternity. Jesus was saying in Mark 11:23-24 that if we are rightfully connected to Him, our faith can release incredible mountain-moving realities. Let's look at five Incredible Mountain-Moving Realities that faith can bring to our lives!

I CAN PROMISE THAT YOU'LL NEVER GET WHAT YOU DON'T ASK FOR

Reality #1:
Faith can enable you to overcome the obstacles in your life!

Do you have any problems, obstacles or challenges facing you today? What do you need from God? The answer is to come to Him in faith, pouring out your desires and trusting Him to help you overcome. I can't promise you that He will always give what you asked for. But I can promise that you'll never get what you don't ask for. James 4:2 says, "You do not have because you do not ask God." When you've got obstacles in front of you, ask God for His help to overcome!

I recently heard a story about a small congregation in the foothills of the Great Smokies that built a new sanctuary on a piece of land willed to them by a church member. Ten days before the new church was to open, the local building inspector informed the pastor that the parking lot was inadequate for the size of the building. Until the church doubled the size of its parking lot, they would not be able to use the new sanctuary. Unfortunately, with its undersized parking lot, the church had used every inch of its land except for the mountain against which it had been built. In order to expand the parking, they would literally have to move some of that mountain out of the back yard.

Undaunted, the pastor announced the next Sunday morning that he would meet that evening with all the members who had "mountain moving faith." They would hold a prayer meeting and ask God to somehow remove the mountain from the back yard and to provide enough money to have the required parking lot paved and painted before the scheduled opening dedication service the following week.

REMEMBER, GOD'S

DELAYS ARE NOT

NECESSARILY GOD'S

DENIALS

At the appointed time, 24 of the congregation's 300 people assembled for prayer. They prayed for nearly three hours. At 10:00 PM, the pastor said the final "Amen," and added, "We'll open next Sunday as scheduled. God has never let us down in the past and I believe He will be faithful this time too." Now, how was God going to do that?

The next morning, as the pastor was working in his study, there came a loud knock at his door. When he called, "come in," a rough looking construction foreman appeared, removed his hard hat as he entered and said, "Excuse me, Pastor. I'm from Acme Construction Company over in the next county. We're building a huge new shopping mall over there and we need some fill dirt. Would you be willing to sell us a chunk of that mountain behind your church? We'll pay for the dirt we remove and pave all the exposed area free of charge, if we can have it right away. We can't do anything else until we get the dirt in and allow it to settle properly."

And sure enough, that little church was dedicated the next Sunday, as originally planned, with the mountain moved and the parking lot intact. Faith can help you overcome your obstacles!

Reality #2:
Faith can keep you steady in the storms of life!

Faith doesn't keep me from every storm, but faith can keep me steady in every storm. Jim Eller, a young man who attends the church I pastor, encountered a severe storm in his life in the spring of 2001. Having suffered a 20-foot fall in a tragic construction accident, Jim is now a paraplegic and confined to a wheelchair. And it's only through his faith in God that Jim has been able to stay steady through this devastating storm in his life. Jim knows he has suffered a blow in the non-guaranteed category of life, his health. But his faith is anchored to those guaranteed categories. He's going to walk again. However, it will most likely be when he gets his new body upon his arrival in heaven. So he doesn't let the disappointment of today keep him from anchoring his hope, by faith, to what's coming up ahead. All of God's promises will be fulfilled in Jim's life.

Right now, while he's waiting for that fulfillment, Jim lives by 2 Corinthians 1:24 which says, "It is by faith you stand firm!" When a storm comes, I need God's peace when I'm tempted to panic. When a storm comes, I need God's strength and stability when I'm tempted to stumble. I need His assurance in place of my fear. Faith in God empowers me to stay steadfast in the storms of life and to trust God to lead me step-by-step until I make it home.

Reality #3:
Faith can release God's provisions to your prayers!

Faith, of necessity, means you believe that you have received what hasn't come to you materially yet. So there can always be a time of unrest when you are in faith's waiting room. When you're there, remember that God's delays are not necessarily God's denials. And remember that if He doesn't give you exactly what you asked for, it's usually because He has something better in mind.

David Livingston was a great missionary to Africa a century ago. He not only brought the good news of God's love and forgiveness to the natives of that vast continent, but he lived it as well, giving him great favor in the hearts of the people. After he felt that God had called him to go deeper into the jungle to take the message of Jesus Christ to those who had never heard it, Livingston encountered a remote tribe of the Congo. He learned that, according to custom, he was to first call for an audience with the tribal chief before entering the village. Failure to comply could have cost him his life.

THE CHIEF EMERGED FROM HIS TENT AND MADE HIS WAY SLOWLY TOWARD THE MAN OF GOD WHOM HE HAD HEARD SO MUCH ABOUT

Livingston was required to wait outside the village with all his possessions lined up next to him. The chief, as a sign of acceptance, would take whatever he desired from among the missionary's possessions. To complete the exchange, the chief would give the guest something of his own. Then, and only then, would Livingston be authorized to enter and share the gospel.

The scene resembled an orderly garage sale. Livingston had set out his Bible, writing pad, clothes, shoes, blanket and his goat. He suffered from a weak stomach that required him to drink goat's milk on a daily basis. Since the local drinking water was often questionable, this was his answer to survival. Often Livingston had asked God to heal his infirmity, but it seemed he was sentenced to drinking goat's milk every morning for the rest of his life.

After what seemed an eternity to Livingston, the chief emerged from his tent and made his way slowly toward the man of God whom he had heard so much about. Ornately attired in ivory and gold, the chief was followed closely by his advisors and priests. He surveyed the possessions of the missionary, while Livingston silently prayed, "Lord, let him take anything he wants except the goat! You know I need its milk for my very survival. Lord, blind his eyes to the goat!"

Now, how would you expect God to answer that prayer? You'd probably think that if God were listening to that prayer and it was prayed in faith, He'd cause the chief to pass over the goat, right? But Livingston didn't know at that point that God had something better to give him. So you can imagine his shock, when no sooner had he prayed than the chief promptly walked over to the goat and pointed at it. One of the chief's advisors whisked the animal away while Livingston stood there stunned, his life seemingly over.

A few moments later, the man who had taken his goat returned. In exchange, he handed Livingston a stick and left. "A stick?" Livingston cried out in disbelief. "This is ridiculous! He takes the one thing I need for my survival and in return I get an old stick!"

A man standing close by, seeing Livingston's confusion, quickly spoke. "Oh no! That is not a stick. My friend, that is the chief's very own scepter. With it you can gain entry to every tribe and village in the interior. You have been given safe passage and great authority as a gift from the king!" Which, when you think about it, he needed far more than he needed his goat. Without the safety and authority of the chief's scepter, he would have been a dead man anyway, which would have likewise cured him of his need for the goat.

As he stood there in awe, Livingston realized the incredible power and wisdom of God's leading. Instead of giving him exactly what he had prayed for, God had given him something much better. From that time forward, the good news of Jesus Christ spread to thousands and thousands of native people. And, as a side note, Livingston's stomach ailment was healed too! [2]

Faith will release God's provisions to your prayers. But it's important after you've prayed to say, "Now Lord, by faith I'm expecting you to give me what I've prayed for, unless you, in your wisdom, have a better plan!"

Reality #4:
Faith can bring healing to your hurts!

The whole area of healing can often be a very confusing topic, particularly when it comes to what effect, if any, faith has on specific outcomes in this area of our lives. I personally believe factors concerning our health are more open-ended than we may think. Even doctors understand this.

I heard about one man who had endured a terribly lengthy surgery. It was expensive and results weren't very promising. He went to his doctor for the post-op visit, and the doctor said, "Well, I have some sad news for you. You're not going to live more than six months." The distraught man said, "Good night, doctor. It's going to take me at least a year just to pay you back what I owe." Whereupon the doctor said, "Well, I'll give you a year then." You understand: we have some control to determine outcomes, but not complete control.

When it comes to healing in our lives, there are three important dimensions to consider. First, there is the issue of physical healing, which is very complex. Here, God often uses the natural means of doctors and medicines and the natural healing process of time. At other times, He adds His supernatural touch to the natural process and does something that goes above and beyond what the doctors and medicines can do, and may even speed up the time process in healing. At other times, more rare, are those moments when He chooses to heal completely apart from the doctors and medicines, and speeds up the time so that there is more of a spontaneous healing. He may use any, or all, or various combinations in bringing about physical healing.

In August of 2001, I had knee surgery to clean up a partially torn meniscus in my knee. I had prayed for God to heal it on His own if He wanted to spare me the medical costs. But eventually I had to have it surgically repaired. Today, God has answered my prayer as my knee has returned to normal. He just used the natural process to do it.

Several years ago, I had a similar situation with my wrist that needed surgery. In fact, I had even checked with the doctor as to the cost for outpatient surgery to have a painful cyst removed. While I was making a decision about it, I happened to tell a Christian friend about it and she said, "Well, why don't we just ask God to heal it." I had to admit, I hadn't even considered that option. So I decided that I was going to take some time to seek God for healing and let Him show me how He wanted me to handle it.

THE HOPE THAT YOU NEED IS A HOPE THAT GOES BEYOND THIS LIFE AND GUARANTEES THAT HEAVEN WILL BE YOUR HOME

Incredibly, within a week of praying about it, that cyst had been reduced to nearly nothing. Another week later and it was completely gone (and, praise God, has been like new ever since). Now I just love it when God says, "Okay, I'm going to do it all by myself!" He does that sometimes and we need to earnestly seek Him for that. But then sometimes, we don't get the physical healing we desire in spite of our prayers and even the doctor's best efforts. When the category is potential rather than positional, we often have to bow to the mystery of why God moves one way one time and a different way the next time . . . why He heals sometimes and at other times He doesn't.

But beyond physical healing is the internal healing of the soul, where God is always at work regardless of what is happening on the physical front. I always know that He wants to work internally in my heart. Not long ago, I discovered a need for some internal healing in my heart stemming from an intense disappointment in my life when I was 20-years-old. I felt like God had let me down and as a result, I had developed a rather cynical edge in my faith which was now keeping me from trusting God as completely as I should. So I was able to present that to God and undergo some internal healing that I needed.

And then, beyond internal healing, is ultimate healing. This is the healing I will receive one day when I pass on to heaven. On June 3, 2001, my sister, Carol, died of breast cancer even though we had prayed many times over the course of several years for her healing. As I grieved her death, what gave me hope and comfort through my tears was the knowledge that though she hadn't been healed physically, she had been healed ultimately and is even now, in heaven, enjoying perfect health! Faith can heal my hurts, but I have to remember that God's healing takes place on several different levels, the greatest of which is His ultimate healing.

So if you have a hurt that needs healing, pray and enlist others to pray for you. God may heal you physically. While you're waiting on Him to do that, He will more than likely do some internal healing. And then, most importantly, is having the assurance that you will be healed ultimately because you have put your faith and trust in Jesus Christ!

Reality #5:
Faith can bring salvation to your soul!

The greatest gift you can ever receive is to know that you have received salvation, to know that your sins are forgiven and that heaven is going to be your home when you die. Overcoming obstacles, staying steady in a storm, receiving provision through prayer and healing for hurts are all related to navigating life on this earth. But the hope that you need is a hope that goes beyond this life and guarantees that heaven will be your home.

We're living in uncertain times. September 11, 2001, changed everything and today the threat of terrorism hangs over our country. Anxiety is running high. We wonder, are we really safe as a country? Where can we find security? Friend, true security is found through faith in Jesus Christ. True security is having the same inner assurance as was spoken of by the apostle Paul in 2 Timothy 4:18 when he said, "The Lord will rescue me from every evil attack and will bring me safely to his heavenly kingdom." That's security!

So I can speak to the mountain of anxiety and fear in Jesus' name and tell it to be thrown into the sea. I know I'm invincible until Christ's purposes for me are through, and then the good part is just starting because I get to go home! Do you know that kind of security in your life today? Have you received God's gift of salvation by faith in Christ?

The only way you can receive that gift is by faith. It's not something you can earn by being good enough. And you don't get it by being moral enough or religious enough. There's only one way: faith in Jesus Christ. Faith in what He has done for you. Religion is spelled D-O. Christianity is spelled D-O-N-E! Christ has already done everything that needs to be done in order for you to receive the free gift of salvation. You simply have to surrender your life to Him and, by faith, ask Him to forgive your sin and to give you eternal life. And having trusted Him for that, you then follow Him by faith the rest of your life.

You talk about moving a mountain! Faith can remove your sin and guilt and get you to heaven. It can give you the best of both worlds. It can enable you to overcome your obstacles, keep you steadfast in a storm, bring God's provision to your prayers and healing to your hurts. That's all great right now. But by far, the vast majority of your life is going to be lived somewhere other than on this earth. By faith, you can make sure that you have life with Jesus for eternity when this life is over. Do you know for sure that you have that today? You can, if you'll reach out and take it by faith. Why not use the following prayer to open your life to Jesus Christ right now, by faith.

Lord Jesus, when I understand what you want to do in my life through faith, I don't want to wait another minute to get started living at a higher level. I open my life to you right now, and invite you into my life. Please forgive my sins and give me your salvation and forgiveness. Help me now, to grow in my faith so that I can follow you faithfully the rest of my life and experience all that you want to release in my life by faith. In Jesus name, Amen.

So far we've talked about the vital importance of faith for our lives and the incredible potential faith can release in us. And hopefully, by now, you're excited about learning more concerning how you can live at a higher level of faith in your life. But like building a skyscraper, or any multi-story complex, the higher you intend to build, the more secure and stable the foundation needs to be. The same is true in building our faith. We need to make sure our faith is resting on a firm foundation. That's the topic of our next chapter.

✿

CHAPTER THREE

"Trust in the Lord with all your heart, and lean
not on your own understanding. In all your ways
acknowledge Him, and He will make your paths straight."
PROVERBS 3: 5-6

LAYING A SURE FOUNDATION FOR FAITH

Those who know me well will not find it difficult to believe that, as a child, I could sometimes be a bit of a handful. It seems I was just wired to pull a lot of crazy shenanigans, often with no explanation for them. Take, for instance, the night soon after I had seen the Tarzan show over at my Grandpa and Grandma's house (we didn't have our own TV until I was in the sixth grade). I was playing with my younger brother, Donnie, in the living room and came up with the brilliant idea that we should play Tarzan.

So there he was in his little Buster Browns (he was probably all of 5-years-old at the time), and I said, "Hey, Donnie! Get down on your hands and knees and then sort of put your head down between your knees with your rump up in the air. I want to act like Tarzan and jump over you."

He knew me all too well and said, "No, you're going to kick me."

In my most convincing voice I said, "No, I won't. I promise." (Yeah right).

Silly Donnie. He actually believed me! I got a good running start, came flying across that living room, and promptly punted him like a football. A moment later, he was lying on the living room floor crying and whining, "You promised you wouldn't kick me!"

I smugly proclaimed, "Yeah, but I didn't mean it. I was just kidding." Needless to say, he never played Tarzan with me again. My Tarzan stunts aside, we've all had experiences in life that have served to remind us that sometimes, when we trust people, we get burned. You've heard the little saying: *Fool me once, shame on you. Fool me twice, shame on me.* We've learned that we have to be on guard lest we become easy prey for people who make promises to us and then, having secured our trust, punt on their promises. You get hurt deeply one too many times and it's as if you learn to go through life with your defenses up in the trust area. We say, "From here on out, I won't trust anybody again."

That presents a real barrier when it comes to cultivating a life of faith in God. Because with Him, it's all about trust. Some of the earliest Bible verses I learned were Proverbs 3:5-6: "Trust in the Lord with all your heart, and lean not on your own understanding. In all your ways acknowledge Him, and He will make your paths straight."

SOMETIMES, WHEN

WE TRUST PEOPLE,

WE GET BURNED

The promise at the end of that passage is that He will direct your life in the right way. "He will make your paths straight." But, that's true only if you trust Him. It's the foundational requirement of a relationship with God: *you've got to trust Him.* He asks us to make a high stakes, faith gamble that if we trust Him, He will prove trustworthy.

What God is asking from us is much like what occurred on a television program preceding the 1988 Winter Olympics where blind skiers were featured being trained for slalom skiing. Paired with sighted trainers, the blind skiers were taught on the flats how to make right and left turns. When that was mastered, they were taken to the slopes. There the sighted partners skied beside them shouting, "Left!" and "Right!" As they obeyed the commands, they were able to negotiate the course and cross the finish line, depending solely on the sighted skiers' word. It was either complete trust or catastrophe.

That is such a vivid picture of how God asks us to live life with Him. In this world, we are, in essence, blind to spiritual realities apart from His guidance. Hence, we must rely solely on the Word of the only One who can truly see things as they are - God himself. And that brings us face-to-face with huge trust issues. Do I believe God is inherently trustworthy or do I believe that if I trust Him, He'll punt on His promises, and then say, "Just kidding!"

As for me, there are few subjects I feel more strongly about than God's trustworthiness. I have banked my life on it. The whole direction, focus and purpose of my life today are based on one central tenet: I believe God is inherently trustworthy, that His Word is true and His promises are sure. He's not going to induce me to trust Him and then, having secured my trust, punt me across the room and say, "I was just kidding. Fooled you!"

IN THIS WORLD,

WE ARE BLIND TO

SPIRITUAL REALITIES

APART FROM

HIS GUIDANCE

But perhaps you aren't so sure about that. So let me ask you: Have you ever stepped out and trusted God and been let down? Have you ever honestly stepped out and obeyed His Word and not found it to be true? When has God ever been unfaithful to you? When has He ever lied to you? Do you really think He would?

Oh sure, I have had moments in my life when I questioned why He was allowing certain things to happen to me that I didn't particularly appreciate or understand. But in those moments I've been forced to realize afresh that God never promised that trusting Him would keep me from the bumps and bruises of real life. He did promise He'd never leave me or forsake me, no matter what. He did promise to strengthen me. He did promise to provide for me. He did promise to give me peace. I have tasted of His trustworthiness in my own life over and over again. Not once has He said, in response to my faith and trust, "Just kidding."

If you're going to walk with God by faith, you can't get away from the issue of trust. So I want to deal with two critical factors in the trust development department of your life in hopes of helping you take some steps to trusting God more fully, regardless of where your trust level is today.

GOD NEVER PROMISED THAT TRUSTING HIM WOULD KEEP ME FROM THE BUMPS AND BRUISES OF REAL LIFE

Faith's Two Foundational Building Blocks!

There are two primary hurdles we must get over if we're going to develop a relationship with God. They are: (1) What do I believe about God's character and (2) What do I believe about God's Word? There's no way to walk with Him by faith, without jumping these hurdles.

#1: Can I trust God's Character?

Do I believe that God would lie to me or make a promise and not keep it? Do I believe that He induces people to trust Him, only to pull the rug out from under them when they do?

There's an old story of a father who took his young son and placed him on the railing of the back porch one day. The dad then went down, stood on the lawn, and encouraged the little fellow to jump into his arms. "Come on, just jump! I'll catch you," the father assured him.

After a lot of coaxing, the reluctant son finally made the leap. When he did, the father stepped out of the way and let him crash to the ground. Picking up the tearful little guy, the father dusted him off and warned him, "Let that be a lesson to you. Don't ever trust anyone." Sounds like a nice guy, doesn't he?

Contrast that with an experience Tim Hansel tells about in his book, *Holy Sweat*. One day, he and his son, Zac, were climbing around on some small cliffs out in the country. Suddenly Tim heard his son's voice above him, "Hey Dad! Catch me!"

Tim writes, "I turned around to see Zac, already in the air, headed straight at me. He had jumped and then yelled, 'Hey Dad!' I performed an instant circus act to catch him. We both fell to the ground and for a moment after I caught him I could hardly talk. Finally, when I found my voice again, I asked him: 'Zac, can you give me one good reason why you did that?'"

Zac responded with remarkable calmness: "Sure . . . because you're my dad."

Tim adds, "His whole assurance was based on the fact that his father was trustworthy."[1]

IS HE A FATHER IN WHOM YOU HAVE IMPLICIT CONFIDENCE THAT HE WILL ALWAYS CATCH YOU WHEN YOU JUMP TO HIM?

Let me ask you, which of those two fathers do you find it easier to overlay on to your understanding of your Heavenly Father? Do you think of God as a Father who coaxes you to jump, all the while promising to catch you, and then lets you crash in order to teach you that you shouldn't trust Him? Or is He a Father in whom you have implicit confidence that He will always catch you when you jump to Him?

I want to assure you that the picture of God the Bible paints for us is of this second variety. Titus 1:2 says, ". . . our faith and knowledge are resting on the hope of eternal life, which God, **who does not lie**, promised us." Did you catch that? God, as to His essential nature, cannot lie. He doesn't make promises and break them.

So if you're going to get anywhere with trust development in your life, and lay a sure foundation for your faith, you're going to have to start with making a fundamental decision about the character of God. You need to embrace, as an unwavering conviction in your life, that no matter what happens, God will always be faithful and trustworthy because He can't be anything else. Moreover, you'll need to surrender to Him any unworthy ideas you may have foisted onto Him from your experience with less than perfect humans.

THE LONGER
I LIVE, THE MORE
CONFIDENT I BECOME
THAT WHAT I SETTLED
BY FAITH YEARS AGO
IS TRUE AND SURE

When we liken God to a human image, we are fashioning God after a false image. So surrender to Him any false images you have today and say, "God, I am willing to believe that because you are God, your character guarantees that you cannot lie. And if you cannot lie, then I can trust you to keep your word." That leads to our second consideration.

#2: Can I trust God's Word?

Here I'm referring primarily to His written Word, the Bible. This is huge! I admit that I don't know how to explain everything in the Bible. But the longer I live, the more confident I become that what I settled by faith years ago is true and sure. I know that I'm not going to find out some day down the road that the Bible was just a collection of man's faulty ideas about God that I should have known better than to believe. But understand, while I believe there's good evidence to support the reliability and accuracy of the Bible, ultimately you must settle this issue by faith.

I remember very well the day I settled the fact that if I had to roll the dice, I was going to bet on the Word of God. My decision was not in spite of the evidence, but without all the evidence I might have wished for. I was at a crossroads decision in my life, the implications of which would have a domino effect on the direction of my life. What I decided with regards to the Bible would determine the moral direction of my life, the scholastic direction, the vocational direction . . . indeed my whole life purpose. I was engaged in a huge wrestling match facing this hurdle: Could I trust the Word of God?

I had just finished my freshman year of Bible College. I was training for the ministry and had gone to visit my older brother for a few days. He was working on his PhD. at Purdue University. While together for those days, we engaged in several spirited discussions concerning our differing views with regard to the Bible. At that time in his life, he had pretty well discarded his belief in the Bible as the fully authoritative Word of God. He was smarter than I was and I didn't have the answers to the questions he was

IT'S AS IF GOD HIMSELF CAME INTO MY ROOM AND SPOKE THE WORDS INTO MY HEART

raising about the veracity of God's Word. But I had to admit, his life seemed more fun than mine. And while he wasn't living an immoral life, he didn't seem to be hung up by all the moral restrictions that I had imposed upon myself out of obedience to the Word of God. So I began to ask myself why I was headed down the road I was on if the Bible wasn't all that it purported to be.

By the time I got home from spending time with him, I was on an emotional roller coaster. I remember saying to God, "Lord, if you're Word isn't true, and I can't trust it, then I have no reason to continue going the direction I'm headed with my life. In fact, the ministry is going to be a waste of my time, because I have nothing to teach people if your Word isn't true. If your Word isn't true, I have no reason to live a moral life and keep my dating relationships sexually pure. If your Word isn't true, then I have no reason to do anything but party my life away. If your Word isn't true, then I don't know where I came from, I have no idea why I'm here, and I certainly don't know where I'm going, so I might as well just have fun while I'm here."

The night I arrived home, I was so emotionally upset that I went to bed at 7 o'clock because I was worn out from thinking about the implications of the decision that was staring me in the face. However, I couldn't sleep. Finally, frustrated and near tears after having tossed and turned until 11:00 p.m., I got out of bed and fell onto my knees. I opened my Bible and said, "God, I've got to know that this is your Word."

I KNEW THE EXPERIENCE OF ASSURANCE THAT GOD SPOKE TO MY HEART THAT NIGHT WAS NOT AN IMAGINED THING

And what happened in those next moments remains one of the most sacred and defining moments of my life. As I began to read the passage to which my Bible had fallen open, it's as if God himself came into my room and spoke the words of 1 Peter 1:3-9 into my heart: "Praise be to the God and Father of our Lord Jesus Christ! In his great mercy he has given us new birth into a living hope through the resurrection of Jesus Christ from the dead, and into an inheritance that can never perish, spoil or fade - kept in heaven for you, who through faith are shielded by God's power until the coming of the salvation that is ready to be revealed in the last time. In this you greatly rejoice, though now for a little while you may have had to suffer grief in all kinds of trials. These have come so that your faith - of greater worth than gold, which perishes even though refined by fire - may be proved genuine and may result in praise, glory and honor when Jesus Christ is revealed. Though you have not seen him, you love him; and even though you do not see him now, you believe in him and are filled with an inexpressible and glorious joy, for you are receiving the goal of your faith, the salvation of your souls."

I don't know how long I remained on my knees that night. I do remember, however, that when I got back into bed, I had settled in my heart once and for all that I was going to live and die trusting the Word of God. I knew the experience of assurance that God spoke to my heart that night was not an imagined thing.

Since that night, as I have stepped out and trusted the Bible, it has proven true in my life just as Jesus declared in John 7:17: "If anyone chooses to do God's will, he will find out whether my teaching comes from God or whether I speak on my own."

So no one misunderstands, it's not that everyone will have, or needs to have, the type of crisis experience I had that night on my knees. But I can tell you that if you're going to walk with God, at some moment in your life you will have to decide your answer to the question, "Can I trust the Word of God? Do I believe His Word is true?"

WHILE YOU MUST TRUST GOD'S WORD BY FAITH, IT IS YET A REASONABLE FAITH BECAUSE THERE IS FACTUAL EVIDENCE TO SUPPORT THE BIBLE'S CLAIMS

Let me hasten to add that what I accepted by faith that night has increasingly been corroborated with hard evidence over time. The evidence continues to suggest that, wherever we can test the Bible's accuracy, it rings true to history. That, to me, suggests that maybe I should be a little more cautious about rejecting those accounts in the Bible for which I don't have evidence.

The October 25,1999, issue of *U.S. News and World Report* ran a cover story asking the question: "Is the Bible True?" The sub-title states: "New discoveries offer surprising support for key moments in history."

The author, Jeff Sheler, writes, "In extraordinary ways, modern archaeology has affirmed the historical core of the Old and New Testaments - corroborating evidence from key portions of the stories of Israel's patriarchs, the Exodus, the Davidic monarchy and the life and times of Jesus."[2]

For example, for years many scholars dismissed the stories of David as reigning over a golden time in Israel's history as purely fictitious, since no evidence for his life outside the Bible existed. Until, in 1993, archeologists turned up a basalt stone with an Aramaic inscription on it, from the ninth century B.C. commemorating a military victory by the king of Damascus over the house of David. It was a bombshell, particularly for skeptics who had long argued the lack of evidence for David proved that the Bible was fictitious.

IT IS IMPOSSIBLE THAT HIS SACRIFICE SHOULD BE INSUFFICIENT FOR YOUR SIN

The author adds many other interesting discoveries that shed light on the Bible's accuracy. A couple of intriguing finds from the life and times of Jesus are the bones of a 60-year-old man which bear the inscription, "Joseph, son of Caiaphas." Experts believe these remains are probably those of Caiaphas, the high priest of Jerusalem. He, according to the Gospels, ordered the arrest of Jesus, interrogated him and handed him over to Pontius Pilate for execution.

In 1961, excavations at the seaside ruins of Caesarea Maritima, the ancient seat of Roman government in Judea, turned up a first-century inscription confirming that Pilate had been the Roman ruler of the region at the time of Jesus' crucifixion.[3] Amazing isn't it?

Now admittedly, we don't have empirical evidence outside the Bible for everything that it reports. But so far, wherever the evidence from history can be tested against the Bible's claims, it suggests that the Bible is firmly rooted in history. So, while you must trust God's Word by faith, it is yet a reasonable faith because there is factual evidence to support the Bible's claims. And when you step out and trust God's Word, you add to it, as well, the evidence of your own personal experience that His Word is true.

Can I trust the character of God and can I trust the Word of God? These are the two critical factors in laying a solid foundation upon which to build your faith. Once you've answered those questions affirmatively, some fantastic implications for your life open up to you.

Implication #1:
I don't have to let doubt run my life.

You silence your doubts by standing strongly on the Word of God and keeping your eyes focused on His character. I remember as a younger Christian, having invited Jesus into my life, I would often question whether I was really saved. I felt I had to keep inviting Jesus into my life over and over again just to make sure I really was saved. Finally, I learned to stand by faith in the assurance of His Word, which says in Acts 2:21, "And everyone who calls on the name of the Lord will be saved.

I used to have doubts about whether I was truly forgiven even after I had asked God for forgiveness. Finally, I silenced my doubts when I learned to stand by faith in the finished work of the cross of Jesus Christ. When Jesus Christ cried out on the cross "It is finished," he was declaring that the debt for my sins had been paid in full. You see, if you have put your faith in Christ and

HE SAID, "THIS IS THE GREATEST THING THAT HAS EVER HAPPENED TO ME."

his sacrifice on the cross for your sin, then it is impossible that His sacrifice should be insufficient for your sin. It is equally impossible that God would somehow not forgive you.

It is simply out of the question that you could get to heaven some day only to hear God say, "I know what I promised, but I was just kidding." Spiritual confidence is a matter of trusting the character of God and the Word of God. You don't have to let doubt run your life any longer.

Implication #2:
I can trust God's heart when I can't trace His hand.

No matter what you go through in this life, God is going to keep His side of the bargain

Roger Simms will never forget the date of May 7. He was hitchhiking home from his stint with the army and the heavy suitcase had him tired out. He was anxious to take off that old army uniform once and for all. Flashing the hitchhiking sign to an oncoming car, he lost hope when he saw it was a sleek black Cadillac. But to his surprise, the car stopped and the passenger door opened. Running to the car, Roger tossed his suitcase in the back and thanked the handsome, well-dressed man as he slid into the front seat.

"Going home for keeps?" the driver asked.

"Sure am," Roger responded.

"Well, you're in luck if you're going to Chicago."

"Not quite that far. Do you live in Chicago?"

"I have a business there. My name is Hanover."

They talked about many things. Roger, who was a Christ-follower, suddenly felt a gentle, but firm leading to tell this 50ish, apparently successful businessman about Christ. He kept putting it off, until he realized he was just 30 minutes from his home. It was now or never.

Clearing his throat, Roger said, "Mr. Hanover, I would like to talk to you about something very important." He then began to explain to him the importance of having a relationship with Jesus Christ, what Christ had done to forgive our sins by dying on the cross and being raised to life, and the need for each person to individually and personally accept Christ's provision by faith. Finally, he asked Mr. Hanover whether there was any reason why he would not like to put his trust in Christ.

To Roger's astonishment the Cadillac pulled over to the side of the road. For a moment he thought he was going to be ejected from the car. But incredibly, the businessman said he was convinced he needed Christ in his life, and right there on the side of the road prayed to receive Christ. A few moments later Mr. Hanover dropped Roger off and thanked him. He said, "This is the greatest thing that has ever happened to me."

WE DISMISS THE RELIABILITY OF GOD'S WORD AT OUR OWN PERIL

Five years went by. Roger married, had a two-year-old boy, and began a business of his own. One day, while packing his suitcase for a business trip to Chicago, he found the small, white business card Mr. Hanover had given him five years earlier. Roger decided that while in Chicago, he would look him up. Arriving at Hanover Enterprises, Roger asked for Mr. Hanover and was informed by the receptionist that while it would be impossible to see Mr. Hanover, he could see Mrs. Hanover if he wished.

A little confused as to what was going on, he was ushered into a lovely office and found himself facing a pretty woman in her fifties. She extended her hand. "You knew my husband?" she inquired.

Roger shared with her how her husband had given him a ride when he was hitchhiking home after the war.

"Can you tell me when that was?"

How could he forget? "It was May 7," he replied, "five years ago. It was the day I was discharged from the army."

Then she asked him, "Anything special about that day?"

Roger hesitated. Should he mention the fact that he had shared Christ with Mr. Hanover and the fact that he had received Christ along side the road that day? Did she not know about this? Where was she spiritually? Finally he decided that since he had come so far, he might as well take the plunge and just share the story.

No one has ever turned to Christ for salvation and been denied

He said, "Mrs. Hanover, I'm a Christian and that day I just felt really compelled to tell your husband about Christ and to challenge him to put his personal trust in Jesus. Incredibly, when I had done this, he pulled over to the side of the road and wept against the steering wheel while he invited Christ into his life. It was fantastic. And I still remember his final words to me: 'This is the greatest thing that's ever happened to me.'"

Before he could finish, Mrs. Hanover was overcome with explosive sobs. After several minutes, finally able to compose herself, she said, "I had prayed for my husband's salvation for years. I believed with all my heart that God would save him."

"And..." said Roger, "so where is your husband now, Mrs. Hanover?"

"He's dead," she wept, struggling to get the words out. "He was in an accident on May 7th, five years ago, apparently sometime soon after letting you out of the car. He never made it home. But you see," she added, sobbing uncontrollably, "I thought God had not kept His promise, so I rebelled against Him and stopped living for Him five years ago because I thought He had not kept His word."

No matter what you go through in this life, God is going to keep His side of the bargain. The Bible says in 2 Corinthians 1:20, "For no matter how many promises God has made, they are 'Yes' in Christ." You may not always see His "yes" but He is never going to break a promise to you. More of your prayers are being answered than you'll ever know. So persevere. Don't turn away from Him in tough times. He will always prove faithful!

Implication #3:
I don't have to leave my eternity to chance.

A man who lived on Long Island was able to satisfy a lifelong ambition one day by purchasing a very fine barometer for himself. When the instrument arrived at his home, he was extremely disappointed to find that the indicator needle appeared to be stuck, pointing to the sector marked "HURRICANE." After shaking the barometer vigorously several times, he sat down and wrote a scathing letter to the store from which he had purchased the instrument. The following morning, on the way to his office in New York, he mailed the letter. But as luck would have it, that very afternoon a huge hurricane did sweep in on Long Island and he lost both his barometer and his home. The barometer's needle had been right all along. He just hadn't heeded the warning.

We dismiss the reliability of God's Word at our own peril. And particularly is this true when it comes to the warning indicators of His Word with regard to our eternal destiny. God has said, "There's only one way to come to me. You have got to embrace my Son who died to forgive your sin."

Many people are just rolling the dice, taking the chance that God really doesn't mean what He says about hell. He's a good guy.

He'll just sort of let anyone in regardless of whether they trusted Him or not. Many think, "God will grade on the curve and I'll be okay!" But the Bible says that no matter how good your own personal record, it's not good enough for a holy God, who cannot just wink at our sin and our mistakes. You need someone who can change your record, erase your violations, cover your mistakes and make you acceptable to a Holy God. Jesus Christ is the Someone whom God himself has chosen.

He absorbed your punishment on the cross. He erases sin and cleanses your mistakes. He offers you a clean slate. At some point you must trust what He did for you rather than trusting what you can do for yourself. There must be a trust transfer for you to gain eternal life. When you trust Christ for your eternal destiny, He will prove Himself to be trustworthy. No one has ever turned to Christ for salvation and been denied. And, trust me, you won't be denied either if you turn to Christ in faith. Open your heart to Him and prove Him to be trustworthy. Not only will He save you, but He will also transform you.

The great news is that once you trust Christ for your eternal destiny, you'll discover that His trustworthiness doesn't end there. He can also help you build a marriage, improve relationships, handle money, resolve conflict, overcome anxiety, deal with anger and find wisdom.

It all comes down to this: Will you trust His character and will you trust His Word? God says to each one of us: "Trust me and I will prove myself faithful. I will direct your life in ways that will fulfill you, challenge you, motivate you, inspire you and satisfy you, both now and for eternity." The question is: Will you trust Him?

Father, I thank you that you are inherently trustworthy and that your Word is true. Please teach me how to trust you with all my heart and to lean more fully upon your Word. As of today, _____(date), I want to go on record that I have decided, by faith, that when forced to decide between your Word and man's opinion, I am going to believe and obey your Word! Thank you that you are a God who cannot lie and because of that, I am released to trust you fully!

Now, having laid a sure foundation for your faith, you're ready to build a deeper faith. We'll talk about how to do that in the next chapter.

CHAPTER FOUR

*"Faith comes by hearing, and
hearing by the Word of God."*
ROMANS 10:17

DEVELOPING A DEEPER FAITH

God's desire is to deepen and strengthen our faith and He deploys all sorts of unique experiences and circumstances in our lives to that end. One of my all-time favorite faith-building experiences revolved around what I call "the mystery of the missing ball glove."

It was the summer of 1978. I was serving as a counselor at our church camp in Lawton, MI, appropriately named "Miracle Camp" in light of some of the things that happened there that summer. This particular week, I happened to be leading a group of fifth and sixth grade boys who arrived on Sunday evening.

I think it was about Tuesday evening when one of the guys mentioned that his ball glove was missing. That night, as we were having a short prayer time before bed, one of the boys got the bright idea that we should pray about finding that lost ball glove (apparently fifth and sixth graders haven't lived long enough in the real world to understand that God has more important things to do than help them find a lost ball glove). But we prayed about it and I figured that would be the last we'd hear about it. It was no big deal if we did or didn't find it. I mean, why not just buy a new one?

The next morning our Bible study centered on God's promise in John 14:14, "You may ask me for anything in my name, and I will do it." The Bible study booklet happened to ask a question about how the kids could apply this to their lives and sure enough, the boy with the lost ball glove says, "Well, I think that means God will help me find my ball glove if we ask Him to." All the other kids thought there seemed to be some connection too. But, I have to tell you, I was a Bible College student and I was sitting there thinking, *Lord, what do I tell them? Am I supposed to tell them that they can't take the Bible quite that literally because otherwise they might end up getting disappointed if they don't find the ball glove? And not only that, but if you don't come through, then they're going to think your Word is untrustworthy.*

IF YOU DON'T COME
THROUGH, THEN
THEY'RE GOING TO
THINK YOUR WORD
IS UNTRUSTWORTHY

Finally, recognizing that I was the only one in the circle who lacked faith, I said, "Okay guys! Let's trust God to help us find that ball glove." And then, based upon His promise, we prayed again and that was that - at least for the kids. I was a mess the next couple of days. Wednesday came and went, no ball glove. Thursday came and went, no ball glove. With my every waking moment I was praying, "Come on God, you've got to pull through for these kids. Show me where that ball glove is!" Now we're down to Friday and the kids leave on Saturday. And I'm pleading, "Lord, show me that ball glove!"

I remember it as if it happened yesterday. We were playing volleyball on a court that used to sit along the lakefront. These kids would blast the ball off their fists and consequently it would spend about as much time in the water as on the court. I'd probably retrieved the ball from the lake two or three times already. But then, one of the kids really clobbered the ball and sent it about 20 yards out into the lake in 2 1/2 to 3 feet of water. This time I waded out, and as I did, the ripples in the water from my movement kept sending the ball a little bit further out as I approached it.

Finally, when I came to the place where the ball was and reached out to get it, there three feet down, lying directly below where that ball was resting, was the ball glove! I was dumbfounded, not only by the fact that God had answered our prayer, but also by the lengths to which He had gone in orchestrating the finding of that glove. I was like, "Oh yeah, why didn't I think to search the lake floor? Of course!"

I was grinning from ear-to-ear when I held up that dripping wet ball glove and said, "Hey guys! Look at this!" And I doubt that any of them has forgotten that specific answer to prayer. I know my faith grew as a result! But as I think about that experience today, contained within it are several of the means by which God deepens our faith. Let's note several of these keys to developing a deeper faith.

> ONCE GOD'S WORD IS QUICKENED IN OUR HEARTS BY THE SPIRIT OF GOD, THEN FAITH COMES ALIVE AND WE PLACE OUR TRUST IN CHRIST

Key #1:
A deeper faith comes by hearing the Word of God!

You see, it wasn't until we were studying the Bible together that God seemed to quicken a particular promise from His Word to our specific situation - finding a lost ball glove. It was then that our faith to trust Him for that answer was activated. God led us to that promise and the Spirit seemed to say, "Trust me to do this." Now, all of a sudden, we began to pray in faith that God would help us find that ball glove.

It's one of the cardinal principles of faith development. I list it first because of its importance. Romans 10:17 says (and I like the way I first learned it in the old King James Version), "Faith cometh by hearing, and hearing by the Word of God." That's the only way anyone ever comes to faith in Christ in the first place and trusts Him to forgive their sin and give them eternal life. We first must hear the message about Christ. Once that message is quickened in our hearts by the Spirit of God that, yes this is the truth and I need to respond to it, then faith comes alive and we place our trust in Christ.

But that is also the way we continue to grow in our faith after we put our trust in Christ. *"Faith cometh by hearing, and hearing by the Word of God."* I have never believed God for anything apart from His Word first being quickened in my heart. And His Word can't be quickened in my heart unless I listen to it and read it with the intent to hear, understand and obey. This is why it's so important that each of us continually prays for an increased appetite for God's Word.

THE TRUTH IS WE ALWAYS MAKE ROOM FOR THAT WHICH WE HAVE AN APPETITE

Mike Benson shares an experience that most parents have had at one time or another. Six green beans sat on his daughter's plate, untouched. Of course, when he said, "Eat your green beans," his 8-year-old daughter said, "Dad, I'm full to the top."

"You won't pop," he responded.

"Yes, I will pop!" she said.

"Risk it. It'll be okay."

"Dad, I couldn't eat another bite if I wanted to."

Mike knew they were having her favorite dessert, so he asked, "How would you like two pieces of pumpkin pie with whipped cream on top?"

"That sounds great," Miss "Ready-to-Pop" answered.

Whereupon Mike asked her the question we've all asked a hundred times: "How can you have room for two pieces of pumpkin pie with whipped cream on top, and not have room for six little green beans?"

Mike says she stood up from her chair and, pointing to one side of her stomach, said, "This is my vegetable stomach." Pointing a little further over, she explained, "Over here is my meat stomach. They are both full." Pointing to the other side of her stomach she said, "Here is my dessert stomach. It is empty. I am ready for dessert!"[1]

The truth is we always make room for that which we have an appetite. Thus, when it comes to faith development, we need to ask God to give us an insatiable appetite for His Word so that we can grow in our faith. Knowing His Word and growing in His Word are critically important to our survival as Christians!

In fact, the Bible likens God's Word to a sword. It's your sword for defending yourself against Satan's attacks and lies. It's your means to walking in peace and security when the world around you is falling apart. You've got to keep your sword in hand so you can battle anxiety and fear.

Some time ago, I heard about an article from the U.S. government Peace Corps' manual for its volunteers who worked in the Amazon jungle. It gives directions on how one is to react if attacked by an Anaconda snake. Keep in mind that the Anaconda is one of the largest snakes in the world. A relative of the Boa Constrictor, it can grow up to 35 feet long and can devour a 300-400 pound animal. This is what the manual said:

If you are attacked by an Anaconda . . .

- Don't run, the snake is faster than you are.
- Lie flat on the ground, put your arms tight against your sides and your legs tight against one another.
- Tuck your chin in. The snake will come and begin to nudge and climb over your body.
- Do not panic.

- After the snake has examined you, it will begin to swallow you from the feet end - always from the feet end. Permit the snake to swallow your feet and ankles. Again, do not panic.
- The snake will now begin to suck your legs into its body. You must lie perfectly still. This will take a long time.
- When the snake has reached your knees, slowly and with as little movement as possible, reach down, take your knife and very gently slide it into the side of the snake's mouth between the edge of its mouth and your leg. Then quickly, rip upward, severing its head.
- Be sure to have your knife. *(That'd be a good idea, huh?)*

SOME OF US HAD

FAITH TO BELIEVE

GOD FOR FORGIVENESS

AND SALVATION,

BUT WE'VE

STOPPED THERE

The truth is, there are those conditions under which, if you don't have your knife, you just might be in trouble. What we need to understand today is that the Word of God is our knife, our sword, when we are facing Anaconda-like problems in our lives and when we feel like we're being swallowed by our troubles. Hebrews 4:12 says, "For the Word of God is living and active. Sharper than any double-edged sword..." Ephesians 6:17, in a classic passage on the tools God has given us for standing strong in our faith against Satan's deceptive tactics says, "Take the sword of the Spirit, which is the Word of God."

When Satan tempted Jesus, what did He do? He used His sword! Three times Jesus answered the temptations of Satan with the Word of God and said, "It is written." (Then He'd quote the truth of God's Word in the face of temptation). The question is, if Jesus defeated His problems by using God's Word, how much more do you and I need to follow His example?

To that end, we have to keep developing ourselves in the Word. *"Faith cometh by hearing, and hearing by the Word of God."* That's the way we begin the journey of faith, and that's the way we continue. Faith in any area of our lives comes by hearing the Word of God. Some of us had faith to believe God for forgiveness and salvation, and we've done that, but we've stopped there. We haven't developed our faith beyond that point. The only way we can or will is by further development in God's Word. The strength of our faith in any area of our lives can be no stronger than the revelation we receive from God's Word.

For instance, there are people who have more faith to believe God for healing in their lives than do other people. Why? Well, because they are more developed in their faith in that particular area of their lives than are other people. Why? Primarily because they have regularly digested teaching from the Word of the God regarding healing. Does it mean that they're "better" Christians than other people or that God likes them better? No, it's just that they're more developed in their faith in that area and receive accordingly.

YOU CAN'T AGGRESSIVELY TAKE HOLD OF THAT WHICH YOU DON'T KNOW YOU POSSESS

There are others who are more developed in the worship portion of their lives or in prayer. Some are more developed in the giving and financial area. Some are more highly developed than others in the marital or child-raising arena. Wherever you invest time listening to the Word of God and developing your understanding in that particular area of your life, your faith will grow and develop and you'll become more proficient at walking by faith in that discipline.

But here's the point: If you want your faith to be stronger in a certain area, then you must spend concerted effort listening to the

Word of God in that particular area. As God reveals more and more truth to your life, your faith will grow. So where do you wish you had stronger faith? Identify an area and then make a concerted effort over the next year to get more teaching on that topic. Study the Word of God, buy books and read them. Learn from others who have advanced beyond you on that topic. Buy tapes and listen to them. As you take in God's Word, He will reveal fresh insights to you and your faith will grow! *"Faith cometh by hearing, and hearing by the Word of God."*

THE STRENGTH OF OUR FAITH IN ANY AREA OF OUR LIVES CAN BE NO STRONGER THAN THE REVELATION WE RECEIVE FROM GOD'S WORD

If you don't know what the Word of God says, then there's no way you can have faith in that particular area. You will be like the guy who was on a seven-day cruise and took bananas and crackers along to eat. When he ran out, he spent several days doing without food, only to learn when the cruise was over that his ticket had purchased access to as much of the food on board that ship that he cared to indulge in. But he didn't take advantage of what was rightfully his because he didn't know it was. You see, you can't aggressively take hold of that which you don't know you possess. You can be on board the cruise of salvation, but miss out on some of the greatest benefits of that wonderful ride.

That's why you need to grow in your understanding of God's Word. That's why you need to get accustomed to a regular diet of the Word of God, feeding on the promises that He has given. *"Faith cometh by hearing, and hearing by the Word of God."*

Key #2:
A deeper faith comes by acting on the Word of God!

Whereas faith can only enter your heart through hearing the Word of God, faith only comes to fruition and releases the blessings of God in your life if you act upon what you have heard. This is why James 1: 22-25 says, "Do not merely listen to the word and so deceive yourselves. Do what it says. Anyone who listens to the word but does not do what it says is like a man who looks at his face in a mirror and, after looking at himself, goes away and immediately forgets what he looks like. But the man who looks intently into the Word, and continues to do this, not forgetting what he has heard, but doing it - he will be blessed in what he does."

The fact is you can know what the Bible says about how to have a better marriage, how to develop your prayer life, how to experience God's supernatural response to giving or how to pray more effectively for the sick. But, until you act on what God has revealed, you are not going to experience the fruit of your faith.

WHEN YOU ACT ON THE WORD OF GOD, YOU WILL BE BLESSED IN WHAT YOU DO

The Bible says in Hebrews 4:2 that those who followed Moses' leadership regularly heard God's Word, "but the message they heard was of no value to them, because those who heard it did not combine it with faith!" Unless we act in faith on what we hear, we are no better off for having heard it. Acting on that word in faith is what activates God's power and blessing in our lives.

Sometimes acting on the Word means we're to rest and quit trying to do what only God can do. When we were praying for that ball glove, the Word of God had led us to ask God to show us where it was. Outside of keeping our eyes peeled for it, there wasn't a whole lot we could do except rest and trust that God would help us find it in His time.

At other times, God's Word will call us to some specific action. Then our obedience is the evidence that we truly have faith. You act on the Word as God gives you further revelation of His will, whether that revelation comes through the preaching of God's Word, your own reading of it or the Holy Spirit prompting you to do something. When you act on the Word of God just because God has told you to act, you will be blessed in what you do. You don't always know exactly what that blessing will look like, but you'll be blessed and your faith will grow because you realize in a new way that God's Word is true.

WE WANT TO ALLOW THE SPIRIT TO LEAD, BUT WE ALSO NEED TO CHECK OUR LEADINGS AGAINST THE WISDOM OF OTHERS

I remember sitting across from a man at a conference in Dallas a few years ago with whom I had been at odds for about three years. I didn't want to be anywhere near him. But God had arranged our being there at the same time and same place. As God's Word was being preached that night, my heart was being broken as He was speaking to me. The Holy Spirit prompted me, "Cal, tonight I want you to repent and ask that man for forgiveness." That was the last thing I wanted to do and I was arguing with God about it. In my heart I was saying, "Lord, if I do that, if I let my guard down, he's going to try and take advantage of me." But God said, "You let me worry about that."

So that night, I went to this man and in tears, I said, "I'm here to repent of my bitterness and anger towards you. Will your forgive me?" And the immediate blessing was the weight of bitterness and hurt that left my heart that evening.

That night we spent several hours talking about the issues that had come between us. And from that moment, we made a commitment to building our relationship with each other. I did not know then, nor could I have imagined the blessing that this man would become to me. He has blessed my wife and I in ways we could not have imagined. In fact, I'm stunned to think of how God has blessed my life through this man. But the point is, the opening to that blessing came through acting upon the Word of God, by faith, even when doing so was the last thing I wanted to do.

Key #3:
A deeper faith comes from following the promptings of the Holy Spirit!

As you sense that God has placed a prompting on your heart and you obey it, your faith grows because of the first-hand experience of how the Holy Spirit leads you.

The Bible says in Romans 8:16, "Those who are God's are led by the Spirit of God." Of course, the more familiar you are with the Word of God, the more readily you'll discern the promptings of the Holy Spirit in your heart. Sometimes, He may bring to mind a particular verse of Scripture in a specific situation. At another time, He may give you a strong sense or compel you to take a certain course of action. And, of course, this might involve a risk. So the riskier you sense the assignment, probably the more you should check out your leading against the wisdom of other, more mature followers of Christ.

You don't want to blame doing something foolish on the leading of the Spirit, unless you are absolutely sure He's asked you to do something foolish! So we want to allow the Spirit to lead, but we also need to check our leadings against the wisdom of others when there's risk involved. And sometimes there will be risk involved.

Having said that, I have often been amazed at what God has done as I've followed His leading, even though I wasn't one hundred percent sure it was His leading at the time. A number of years ago our church was meeting in a renovated truck dock and in desperate need of more office space. We had looked around town for available office space and it was obvious to us that the best-case scenario would have been for us to lease space from the local moving and storage company that sat right next door to our church. But every time we inquired of them, they had nothing available for rent. I still remember pulling up in front of their building one day and saying, "God, we're stuck and this would be so ideal. Please open up a section of these offices for us unless you have better plans?"

Well, nothing opened up and the storage company wasn't holding out hope for anything coming available any time soon, so we moved on and went looking for other space. We were thinking about bringing in a portable unit and were down to the day when we needed to make a decision. And right at the last minute, I remember the clear prompting that came to my heart, "Go back and ask the storage company for space one more time before you do anything." And I almost just waved it off because my mind was telling me, "Cal, you've already been told 'no' more times than you can count, so what's the likelihood that they'll have anything open now? What don't you understand about the word 'no'?"

YOU GET AN ANSWER TO PRAYER AND NOT ONLY WILL YOUR JOY BE FULL, BUT YOUR FAITH WILL INCREASE

So I asked one of our Associate Pastors to go over one more time and check with them. And would you believe it? When he came back, he said, "Cal, they have a bunch of office space coming open and it's all ours." The price we later negotiated was far less than anything else in town. But those offices came as a prompting, even after we had been denied over and over again. And guess what? My faith in God's ability to lead me by His Spirit grew even greater! And, my desire to be led by the promptings of the Spirit grew as well.

Key #4:
A deeper faith comes from receiving answers to prayer!

When you have asked God for something and received His answer, there's nothing that will deepen your faith and also cause you to pray more. Do you think it did something for my faith, and that of those boys, when we found the ball glove that we had been praying for? Do you think the next time we lost something we thought about praying for it? You see, you get an answer to prayer and not only will your joy be full, but your faith will increase.

YOU NEED A GOD WHO IS THERE TO COMFORT YOU WHEN YOU CAN'T STOP THE TEARS

A few years ago, a lady asked me to pray for her baby son. He had a painful condition of wart-like sores all over his body and the doctors were doing their best to contain it. I asked her to bring him to our offices when our staff would be assembled for prayer, because I wanted us all to pray for him. And while we were praying, I felt a "go for it" in my heart and so I spoke directly to the condition and said, "In Jesus name, leave this child."

Do you know that from that day those warts began to dry up and fall off until the baby was completely well? Now the mystery of faith is why God answers so dramatically in one case and not in another. But what I do know is that I have seen enough answers to prayer that I am going to pray until God answers, gives me something better or shows me that I need to be praying for something else. And when He answers, your faith grows.

Max Lucado shares a story about the birth of their first child coinciding with the cancellation of their health insurance. He says, "I still don't understand how it happened. It had to do with the company being based in the U.S. and Jenna being born in Brazil. Denalyn and I were left with the joy of an eight-pound baby girl and the burden of a $2,500 hospital bill. We settled the bill by draining a savings account. Thankful to be able to pay the debt but bewildered by the insurance problem, I wondered, 'Is God trying to tell us something?'

"A few weeks later, the answer came. I spoke at a retreat for a small, happy church in Florida. A member of the congregation handed me an envelope and said, 'This is for your family.' Such gifts were not uncommon. We were accustomed to and grateful for these unsolicited donations, which usually amounted to $50 or $100. I expected the amount to be comparable. But when I opened the envelope, the check was for (you guessed it) $2,500."[2] Now let me ask you something: Do you think Max's faith increased or decreased through that answer to prayer?

When you pray, you put yourself in a place where you might experience an answer to prayer. And when you experience an answer to prayer you begin to realize that God really is involved in the details of your life. Consequently, your faith grows.

Key #5:
A deeper faith comes from enduring tests!

It might be waiting on God to answer a prayer for a lost ball glove when you don't know if He's going to come through or not, or being asked to trust Him during the loss of your job. Maybe it's waiting on Him during the failing of your health or facing some other test or trial that has really put you under pressure. You don't know if you have the ability to endure. It's in times like these that you find God is faithful. Whether you get the answer you're hoping for or not, what you find you need most is a God who is there to carry you when you can't walk anymore. You need a God who is there to comfort you when you can't stop the tears.

People with the deepest and strongest faith today are usually the people who have walked with God through the most severe trials and found that when He was all they had left, He really was all they needed.

It's part of how God grows our faith. He puts us in a hard place to show us that He alone is the one who can sustain us. I Peter 1:6-7 says, "For a little while you may have had to suffer grief in all kinds of trials. These have come so that your faith - of greater worth than gold, which perishes even though refined by fire - may be proved genuine and may result in praise, glory and honor when Jesus Christ is revealed." God wants you to have a genuine faith that will endure until you see Him face-to-face.

He puts us under pressure and brings us to an end in ourselves so that we learn He's big enough to carry us when we can't walk

The only way we demonstrate that our faith is genuine, and the only way it can be refined so that it becomes more genuine, is for us to experience trials and tests that take us to the breaking point. I have not yet experienced a test I enjoyed. But I have always come to appreciate the greatness of God and to trust Him more fully on the other side of the test.

I have never forgotten a staff meeting a number of years ago when I went around the room and asked each staff member to share the time in his/her life when he/she felt the closest to God. Almost without exception, the stories in that room were stories of great trial and severe tests. One guy spoke of being down to his last cent at college and having to completely trust God to provide . . . and He did! As a result, his faith in God's care for him and ability to provide, grew *(I almost decided to quit paying him so he could grow closer to God again)*.

As for me, I shared the time at seminary when my wife and I

were down to 89 cents to our name and wondering how God was going to supply. He did! I shared of losing my son and wondering how God was going to take me through. He did! I shared of those times when I was weakest, because that's when I got to see God's strength the most clearly, and because of that, my faith grew. God puts us under pressure and brings us to an end in ourselves so that we learn He's big enough to carry us when we can't walk. And when we experience His strong arms around us, our faith grows!

From lost ball gloves to tests and trials, God's in the business of developing a deeper faith within us. But remember, whatever method He may use, you can be sure that the Word of God will be central to it, for *"faith cometh by hearing and hearing by the Word of God."*

Lord, Thank you that you are committed to helping me grow in my faith. I now understand that faith comes by hearing, and hearing by the Word of God. To that end, I pray that you would increase my appetite for your Word. Oh Lord, make me so hungry for your Word that I can barely get enough of it. And then, as I understand your Word, help me to act on it, knowing that you bless those who are doers of the Word. Make me a doer of the Word! Help me to discern the promptings of the Spirit as He quickens your voice to my heart. Help me to pray in accordance with your Word, knowing that you always respond to prayers that are in keeping with your Word. And then Lord, help me to stay strong in your Word as I experience trials in my life, knowing that they are sent to strengthen my faith. Please Lord, deepen and grow my faith for your glory and my good. In Jesus name, Amen

I hope you're enjoying the faith journey thus far. I hope you're discovering that growing in your faith is the most exciting adventure in life. But along the way, we'll have to beware of some possible obstacles that could hinder the growth of our faith. We turn to that consideration in the next chapter.

CHAPTER FIVE

"A man's own folly ruins his life,
yet his heart rages against the Lord."
PROVERBS 19:3

OVERCOMING OBSTACLES TO FAITH

As a Southern Gospel music lover, I have always enjoyed a song that was popular a number of years ago about Naaman the leper, a man in the Bible who needed healing from a serious disease. When God told him to go dip in the Jordan River seven times, this song's lyrics said, "Naaman had to learn that when God says 'seven,' six won't do."[1] Just as I had to learn that when the coach says, "in by eleven", twelve won't do.

I was cruising along in my junior year of basketball as one of the leading scorers in the area, and my brother, who was a senior, was the second leading scorer on our team from his guard position. Both of us played for our brother-in-law, which had certain advantages. But it also had its disadvantages, particularly when you broke curfew on the night before a game. When there are strong family connections to the coach, things like that have a way of getting back to him. And it did!

You would have enjoyed the little "inner family" squabble that took place in the locker room between the coach, my brother and me when we learned that he might sit us out for the entire game. We were not happy campers. Even though it cost me only one quarter on the bench, curfew was never an issue for me again. I discovered that I would far rather enjoy the excitement of being on the floor than the misery of the being on the bench, if I had a choice in the matter. I just had to learn that when the coach says "eleven," twelve won't do!

But looking back at that situation in my life and recognizing our human tendency to blame others for our self-imposed misery, I'm reminded of Proverbs 19:3 which says, "A man's own folly ruins his life, yet his heart rages against the Lord." Right? We mess up our own lives and then blame everybody else, including God. And nowhere is that more true than when obstacles of our own making keep us from the great things God would otherwise do in our lives. No one in the Bible personifies that principle more than Naaman. We find his story in 2 Kings 5. It's a story that has much to teach us about removing the obstacles that inhibit our ability to receive God's best for our lives.

Just to familiarize you a little bit with Naaman, the Bible tells us that he was a commander of the army of the king of Aram. Naaman was a very highly regarded military man who had won some great victories for his country. Think of him as something like the Norman Schwarzkopf of his day in his country. However, he had a health problem, a skin disease of some kind, perhaps something akin to leprosy.

Naaman also was an Aramean. The capital of Aram was Damascus in Syria. In other words, he was from among Israel's enemies, pagans who worshiped the false god Rimmon. So if ever there was a man who didn't qualify for receiving something from God, it was Naaman, because he wasn't even on the right team. But then, as now, God delights in responding to anyone who reaches out to Him in faith. The Bible tells us that God is not a respecter of persons.[2] However, He is a respecter of faith!

Apparently, on one Aramean sortie into the northern part of Israel, a young Israelite girl was taken captive and ended up in Naaman's house as a servant to his wife. One day, as she was going about her housekeeping duties, she said to Mrs. Naaman, "You know, if only Mr. Naaman would see the prophet, Elisha, who is in Samaria! Elisha would cure him of his leprosy."

When Naaman heard about this possibility, he was more than willing to try anything. So he quickly saddled up his horse and headed for Samaria, soon arriving with a whole entourage of horses and chariots at the front door of Elisha's house.

Elisha sent his messenger to the door with these simple instructions, "Go wash yourself seven times in the Jordan River, and your flesh will be restored and you will be cleansed." Now that wouldn't seem like a major ordeal, would it? If you want God to heal you of your disease, it will require a simple act of faith: Go dip in the Jordan River seven times.

But incredibly, the Bible says that Naaman went away angry and said, "I thought that he would surely come out to me and stand and call on the name of the Lord his God, wave his hand over the spot and cure me of leprosy. Are not Abana and Pharpar, the rivers of Damascus, better than any of the waters of Israel? Couldn't I wash in them and be cleansed?"

WE MESS UP OUR OWN LIVES AND THEN BLAME EVERYBODY ELSE, INCLUDING GOD

He was saying, "What do you mean dip in that filthy river seven times? Why that thing's dirty! I'm likely to get something worse sloshing around in that stuff." Naaman said, "No way. I'm not going to do it," and off he went in a rage.

Now I find that amazing. Here's a guy who desperately needed what God had to give him and what God wanted to give him. Yet, his unwillingness to comply with the simple "faith conditions" that God had laid out kept him bound in his misery instead of experiencing the blessing of God in his life. That's always our choice as well. God won't make us do anything we don't want to do. But it's the essence of folly to go off in a huff just because we don't like the conditions that God has established. All Naaman needed to do was respond in faith and he'd have received what God had promised.

I assume that many of us are like Naaman in that we have a need and really would like God to do something about it. The first thing I do when I'm at that place of need in my life is to ask the question, *"Am I aware of any obstacles in my life that may be preventing me from meeting the 'faith conditions' that God has asked for?"* And I find in Naaman's story, four common obstacles that act as barriers to our receiving from God. We'll call them **Obstacles That Keep Us From Faith's Reward** because when we have these obstacles in our lives, we're not responding to God in faith.

> IT'S THE ESSENCE OF FOLLY TO GO OFF IN A HUFF JUST BECAUSE WE DON'T LIKE THE CONDITIONS THAT GOD HAS ESTABLISHED

Obstacle #1:
Noncompliance to a clear directive from God!

Parents, we know what it is to deal with noncompliance! We've asked our teenager to clean her room for the umpteenth time and it still looks unfit for human habitation. And then that child has the audacity to come to us and ask, "Can I have so-and-so spend the night with me, or go with so-and-so to the party?" Does an issue of noncompliance ever keep you from giving to your child what you otherwise would give? I think we understand.

And it's very important that we understand this about the Lord. When God issues a directive, He's not waiting for us to vote on whether we like it or not. So in verse 10, Naaman has received very clear instructions: "Go, wash yourself seven times in the Jordan, and your skin will be restored and you will be cleansed." And then in verse 11, those two little words show up that so often get us in trouble: "But Naaman." But Calvin, but Mark, but Mary, but Judy. When God issues a directive, He's looking for a "But Nothing!" When God issues a directive, He wants no "ifs", "ands" or "buts". Excuses don't work with Him. He only blesses the obedience that comes from faith.

That little "But Naaman," reminded me of the Scottish pastor who used this as his text one day for a message: But Naaman! And it literally was one of the most powerful messages he'd ever preached. The response of the people was overwhelming. Now you need to understand that in Scotland, "but" is simply a conjunction, and nothing more. It's not a noun. It's not something you sit on or something you tell others to get in gear.

When God issues a directive, He's not waiting for us to vote on whether we like it or not

Well, he was on a sabbatical to the United States and had been asked to preach one Sunday at a rather large church and thought that he would pull out his, "But Naaman" message, since it had been so well received back at his home church. This time, however, he noticed that the people found it more amusing than convicting. They were snickering and laughing all the way through it and by the end, the Scottish guest was just demoralized.

Later on, when the senior pastor of the church, who had been out of town that Sunday, asked him how it had gone, the Scottish preacher said, "I just don't understand it. God used it so mightily back in Scotland, but here it was as if your people thought it was funny!"

The pastor replied, "That's strange. Give me the nub of what you shared."

"Well," the Scottish pastor said, "my text was taken from

2 Kings 5:11, 'But Naaman . . .' And I basically shared three points: (1) Each of us has a 'but.' (2) Some people's 'buts' are bigger than others. And (3) It's a lot easier to see somebody else's 'but' than it is to see your own." (Sorry, I couldn't resist)!

Now don't let that bit of humor blind you to the real issue. I wonder, in your life today, where that conjunction "but" may be getting in the way of your obeying a very clear directive from God. I have run into many people who say things like, "I know that's what the Bible says, but . . ." "I know what the Bible says about sexual purity, and reserving sex for marriage, but . . . come on this is 2003!" And God says, "If you want me to bless your life and bless you relationally, but nothing!"

Others say, "I know Jesus wants me to get baptized as an expression of my faith in Christ, but . . . I don't think you have to take it that literally." "I know the Bible says I'm to love my wife as Christ loves the Church, but . . . you don't know my wife." "I know the Bible says I'm to renew my mind, but . . . come on, a little fantasy never hurt anyone." "I know the Bible defines a tithe, a tenth of my income, as the starting place for generous giving to the work of God's kingdom, but . . . I have a lot of other needs in my life." And on and on the list could go . . . but, but, but! "Naaman, go down and dip in the Jordan seven times if you want God's blessing on your life. But Naaman . . . went away angry!"

How about you? Is there any place in your life where you may know what God has asked you to do, but . . . your response has been one of noncompliance? You can be assured that as long as that is your response, you're going to miss out on God's best. God's blessing falls where He finds people who will say, "Okay, by faith I'm going to take this step in my life just because it's what God said I'm to do!"

In Romans 1:5, Paul speaks of calling people "to the obedience that comes from faith." Faith is demonstrated by my obedience, my compliance with what God says, wherever I recognize that I am not living in accordance with His Word. And when I come into line with His will, I step under the umbrella of His blessing. So come in out of the rain and step under that umbrella today wherever you know you've been unwilling to comply with something God has said. Noncompliance to a clear directive from God will keep you from faith's reward!

Obstacle #2:
Misconceptions about the way in which God works!

At times I have been troubled by the notion I get from some Christians that seems to imply that God has an obligation to answer us exactly as we have asked Him to. We have to remember that God is infinitely creative in the ways He may move in our lives. Therefore we need to let go of our preconceived notions of what we think He ought to do or our misconceptions about how we think He should do it.

FAITH IS DEMONSTRATED BY MY OBEDIENCE, MY COMPLIANCE WITH WHAT GOD SAYS

Notice in verse 11, one of the obstacles in Naaman's life that kept him from responding in faith to what God had said was a misconception about how he expected God to work in his life. He went away angry and said, "I thought that he [Elijah] would surely come out to me and stand and call on the name of the Lord his God, wave his hand over the spot and cure me of my leprosy." Notice those two critical words, "I thought." Where, in your own mind today, might you be carrying a misconception that is limiting what you are receiving from God because of what "you think" God ought to do?

Now there is nothing wrong with praying as specifically as we can regarding the needs in our lives. But when we've given those needs to God, we need to be able to say as well, "Now Lord, I want only your best and I stand ready to receive your blessing in whatever form that might come and however you want to do it." Many times I have been amazed, after having received an answer to prayer that was quite different from what I had prayed, at how much better God's answer was than what I originally thought I wanted or needed. Have you ever experienced that? You thought you knew what was best, and God disappointed you by not answering your prayer as you thought He should, only to shock you later with something much better.

WE HAVE TO REMEMBER THAT GOD IS INFINITELY CREATIVE IN THE WAYS HE MAY MOVE IN OUR LIVES

I will never forget, having moved to Peoria in 1990, what it was like to look for a home as a first-time buyer. We looked at 10 or 15 different homes before we found one that we really liked, even though it would require a lot of work to fix it up. I have no idea today what I was thinking then, because I have absolutely no talent or inclination for fixing up houses. This house had been on the market for two years and had gone nowhere, which should have told us something. But nonetheless, we liked it and told our realtor that we would think it over for the night and pray about it. We prayed, and said, "God, please give us that house. But if there's some reason you don't want us to buy it, then please show us that as well."

The next day we called our realtor and said, "We've decided we want to buy that house." To our astonishment, she replied, "You aren't going to believe this but it went 'pending' yesterday!" Of course, we were a bit discouraged and questioned the Lord, "God, why did you lead us to that house, and then just at the time we wanted to buy it, have it taken off the market?" That was so frustrating to us, even though that's exactly what we had asked

God to do if He had a better plan in mind. We just hadn't expected a better plan.

Now I can't tell you exactly why God closed the door on that house in answer to our prayer, but I can tell you today I'm so glad He did. Every time I drive by that house today, I just shake my head and say, "Lord, what were we thinking? Thank you for keeping us from making a huge mistake!"

There are a lot of people who, like Naaman, haven't gotten the answer they wanted from God, or perhaps a different answer than they expected, and have walked away in a huff. We say things like, "If God really cared, He would have done this or that. If God really cared, He wouldn't have allowed this or that to happen." The truth is that God really does care, and He cares so much that He doesn't always give us what we think we want or need, simply because He wants to give us something better. We just need to lay down our misconceptions of what we think He ought to do and the way we think He ought to do it, and submit completely to what He wants to do in His own way and time.

> HE DOESN'T ALWAYS
> GIVE US WHAT WE
> THINK WE WANT
> OR NEED, SIMPLY
> BECAUSE HE WANTS
> TO GIVE US
> SOMETHING BETTER

Obstacle #3:
Insistence upon an "instant" answer!

We live in an instant society: instant coffee, instant oatmeal, instant weight loss, instant meals, instant success. Then, when we have a need that calls for us to depend upon God, we want an instant answer.

Naaman was just like us. He says in verse 12, "I thought that he would... wave his hand over the spot and cure me of my leprosy" (I wonder if this is where we get the idea of waving the magic wand over something). What was he saying? "I want the answer to be as quick and easy as possible." Wouldn't we all? But that is not usually God's way. So, some of us get frustrated when God asks us to expend a little bit of energy in helping to secure the answer to our need, or when the answer doesn't come as quickly and easily as we wanted it to. God can work in an instant, but most of the work He wants to do in our lives takes time and usually a good bit of effort on our part.

In an earlier chapter, when explaining about how God works in the healing of physical needs, I mentioned that there are different facets to healing. There is inner healing, spiritual healing, and physical healing. Not only that, but the timing in each case may vary. God sometimes releases instant answers. But more often than not, He orchestrates His answers over time.

One of the more dramatic answers to prayer I've seen happened in the life of a man named Dave a few years ago. Dave was suffering from a muscle disease and was wasting away. His weight had dropped from 185 to 125. He couldn't walk on his own anymore and had developed a huge ulcer, which was keeping him from eating the food and taking the medication he needed in order to get better. I had prayed many times, hoping that God would wave His hand and heal Dave, but to no avail. I was growing discouraged.

One day Dave admitted to me that the root of his ulcer was anxiety related and not due to his disease. He was worried because he knew that should he die from this disease, he was not ready to meet God. Dave knew he had never really placed his faith and trust in Jesus Christ. I asked him if he would like to invite Christ into his life, and there in the middle of his living room floor that day, Dave gave his heart and life to Jesus. Only then ·did I recognize that a far deeper need in his life would have gone unmet had God instantly healed Dave's physical need, as I had asked Him to.

However, with that deeper need now met, I prayed some more

for his physical healing. And to my astonishment, a few days later when I went back to see Dave, I found him sitting in a chair eating pizza! I said, "Dave, what's the deal? What happened to your ulcer? I mean, I don't usually think of ulcers and pizzas as belonging together."

He then recounted for me what had happened in the wee hours of the morning, the day after we had prayed. He had been sitting in his chair at 5:00 a.m. in excruciating pain from the ulcer, when all of a sudden, in an instant, the pain was gone.

A later trip to the doctor confirmed that the ulcer was completely gone. With the ulcer now healed, he could eat whatever he wanted, and as he began to eat, he began to get stronger and eventually was completely healed of the muscle disease. The last I saw Dave he was back up to 185, he was back to work and suffering no ill effects from the disease. But think about it. In Dave's case there had been spiritual healing, inner healing, physical healing, instant healing and healing over time all in one situation.

FAITH REQUIRES THAT WE TRUST IN BOTH THE DETAILS AND THE TIMING OF GOD'S PROVISION

The whole point is that it's fine to ask God for what you need. But to become frustrated because you didn't get an instant answer is to miss out on some of the other work that needs to be done in you that can't be done in an instant. Faith requires that we trust in both the details and the timing of God's provision.

Obstacle #4:
Reliance upon human reasoning!

In verse 12, Naaman begins to do what we so often do: he resorts to human reasoning. *"Well, I don't know why God would want me to have to do this or that, so I'm going to do it a different way."*

Naaman says, "Aren't the waters of Abana and Pharpar better than any of the waters of Israel? Why couldn't I just go dunk myself in them instead?" That's human reasoning.

Naaman could have spent all the time he wanted washing in those rivers, with all different kinds of soap, but that was not going to solve his problem or release God's blessing in his life, because he was trying to secure by human wisdom what only faith could give him. I can't always tell you why God says to do things a certain way. What I do know is that it doesn't work out when we do it our way instead of His! The blessing of God comes to my life when I am able to say, "Lord, I don't understand in my limited human reasoning why you are asking me to do something a certain way. Nevertheless, I believe that in your infinite wisdom you know what is best, so I'll trust you and do it your way."

> WHAT I DO KNOW IS THAT IT DOESN'T WORK OUT WHEN WE DO IT OUR WAY INSTEAD OF HIS!

How often we're like the little 4-year-old boy who was sitting on the front seat of the car trying to tell his mom how to drive. "Come on, Mom, get going!" But he was too little to see that a school bus was stopped in front of them. As soon as they started up he said, "Hurry up, Mom, go around him!" But he was too small to see that there was a double yellow line, prohibiting their passing. And then his mom realized, "How like that I am in my own human reasoning at times, thinking I know more about it than God does."

Perhaps as you're reading this book, you realize that you have not yet become a follower of Jesus Christ. Maybe putting your faith in Him doesn't make sense to you because for you, it's an issue of human reasoning. You might be thinking, "I can just be a good person, and I'll be alright. I'm as good as a lot of people who go to church. Not only that, but who are Christians to think that Jesus Christ is the only way to heaven?"

If it were up to me, I'd tell you that it doesn't matter what you believe so long as you're sincere. But, that's not what the Bible says and my job is to tell you what the Bible says. Like Naaman, you can go off in a huff because you don't like what the Bible says, but I just want you to know that the blessing of God comes when you bow your human reasoning to the Word of God and accept it by faith. Accepting God's Word by faith doesn't mean that you have to leave your brain behind. Use your brain to study the evidence for Christ's claims, and when you do, you'll find that faith in Him makes sense.

MANY PEOPLE MISS OUT ON THE BLESSINGS OF GOD BECAUSE WHAT HE TELLS THEM TO DO DOESN'T MAKE SENSE TO THEIR HUMAN WAY OF THINKING

A lot of good evidence exists to suggest that the historical claims about Jesus Christ set forth in the Bible are both factual and reliable. But once you've done your study you have to make a choice to respond by faith, to trust Jesus Christ and to rely on God's Word as truth.

Human wisdom will not get you into heaven. Sincerity is not enough. Morality is not enough. You can't be good enough, rich enough, smart enough or religious enough. The only way to heaven is through a relationship with Jesus Christ. He said in John 14:6, "I am the way, the truth and the life. No one comes to the Father but by me." Ultimately, that's an issue you have to embrace by faith.

Many people miss out on the blessings of God because what He tells them to do doesn't make sense to their human way of thinking. It's doesn't make sense that "faith in Jesus Christ" should be the only way to heaven. It doesn't make sense that I would do better on 90% of my income by giving 10% to God instead of keeping 100% for myself. It doesn't make sense that my relationships would work better if I did things God's way. But until you bow your mind to God's wisdom, you're never going to experience what He wants to give you!

There is a kind of "faith reasoning" that transcends human reasoning. Here you come to recognize that if God has told you to do something, then the smartest and most reasonable thing you can do, whether you understand it or not or feel like it or not, is to do what God says. And I have yet to find a person who lives by that kind of "faith reasoning" who wouldn't also tell you that it's the smartest decision they've ever made, proven so by the rewards that it's brought to their lives.

Another line in that song about Naaman says, "I know Naaman may have doubted if God's promise would be true, but Naaman had to learn when God wants seven, six won't do!"[3] And if you get nothing else from this chapter, get this: God wants to bless your life and the key to that blessing is simply doing whatever He tells you to do. Lay down your objections and the obstacles that may be keeping you from receiving His blessing in your life, and say, "Okay Lord, you want me to dip seven times, you've got it, even if I look and feel like a dip in the process!"

Verse 14 tells us that Naaman finally came to his senses, went and dipped in the Jordan seven times and came up with skin like a baby. Ask Naaman today and he would likely tell you: "I do things my way and go away mad! I do things God's way and go away glad!" That's your choice as well.

Father, Please incline my heart to obey you fully, no matter what you ask me to do. May you find in me a person who is ready to do your will, no matter how difficult and no matter how fully or how little I may understand why and what you are asking me to do. Just say the word and I will do it, no if's, and's or but's! Wherever you see an obstacle in my life that is restricting the full release of my faith, please remove it from my life. In Jesus name, Amen!

A few years ago, a popular TV commercial asked the question: "How do you spell relief?" The answer: R-O-L-A-I-D-S! Those of you who remember that commercial are really dating yourselves. I have often thought of that old Rolaids ad when I have asked another question: "How do you spell faith?" The answer: R-I-S-K! If you're going to walk by faith, sometimes it will feel like risky business. We turn now to facing the risk factor in faith.

CHAPTER SIX

"I tell you that to everyone who has, more will be given,
but as for the one who has nothing,
even what he was will be taken away."
LUKE 19:26

FACING THE RISK FACTOR IN FAITH

The September 6, 1999, issue of *Time* Magazine, carried a special article on risk-taking entitled, *Life On The Edge*. In this article, there was some discussion as to what makes people want to jump out of airplanes, ride their motorcycles off cliffs and participate in all sorts of high risk adventures. The article noted that, according to American Sports Data Inc., a consulting firm, participation in so-called "extreme sports" is way up. Snowboarding, mountain biking, skateboarding, scuba diving, you name the adventure sport - and the growth curves reveal a nation that loves to play with danger. But so do hospital emergency rooms, as more Americans than ever are injuring themselves while pushing their personal limits.[1]

Now you may have wondered at times, "What possesses a person to want to push the envelope like that?" You may never understand a person who likes to live on the edge. By contrast, you prefer "terra firma," and the firma, the betta. Others of us understand the sentiments of Eric Perlman, a mountaineer and filmmaker who specializes in extreme sports, when he says, "We are designed to experiment or die."[2] Never mind that we may die while experimenting.

I found two features of the article to be rather fascinating. One was the discussion by behavioral geneticists as to the possibility that a thrill-seeking gene predisposes some people to want to push the envelope. Israeli scientists, in studying specific stretches of DNA, found that people who were curious and excitable tend to exhibit longer versions of a gene known as D4DR, than did subjects who were described as laid back and reflective.[3] So, this has given me a valid explanation when my wife is wondering what could possibly possess me to want to bungee jump from 100 feet up! My response now is "Honey, I've got to take my D4DR for a drive."

At the end of the article was a 20-question quiz designed to gauge the range of risk with which we feel comfortable. A score of 16-20 indicated that you're probably just back from hang gliding in the Himalayas. If you scored 10-15, you're a sushi eater who'd skip the trip to Japan. A 5-10 means, "Don't forget the umbrella. It might rain." Finally, a score of 0-5 says, "So, how long have you been in life insurance?"[4]

SOMETIMES LIFE

SIMPLY FORCES

YOU OUT OF YOUR

COMFORT ZONE

I scored a 17, and am ready for that hang gliding trip to the Himalayas. My wife, meanwhile, is telling me to take the umbrella when I go out because it might rain!" If you're a thrill-seeker, you've got that long strand of D4DR and have probably married someone in whom that strand is virtually nonexistent or seriously stunted! That can make for some interesting dynamics in your marriage.

Wherever you are on the risk-taking scale, the truth is that risk is simply a part of life. Try as you might to stay "comfortable," sometimes life simply forces you out of your comfort zone. Larry Laudan, a philosopher of science, has spent the last decade studying risk management. He writes of how we live in a society so fear-driven that we suffer from what he calls *risk-lock* -

a condition which, like gridlock, leaves us unable to do anything or go anywhere. He summarizes literature on risk management in 19 principles. The first principle is the simplest: *Everything is risky.* If you're looking for absolute safety, you chose the wrong species.

You can stay home in bed to avoid risk, but that may make you one of the half-million Americans who require emergency room treatment each year for injuries sustained while falling out of bed. You can cover your windows, but that may make you one of the 10 people a year who accidentally hang themselves on the cords of their Venetian blinds. You can hide your money in a mattress, but that may make you one of tens of thousands of people who go to the emergency room each year because of wounds caused by handling money - everything from paper cuts to (for the wealthy) hernias.[5]

Try as we might, we cannot eliminate risk from life. Eileen Guder wrote, "You can live on bland food so as to avoid an ulcer, drink no tea, coffee or other stimulants in the name of health, go to bed early, stay away from night life, avoid all controversial subjects so as never to give offense, mind your own business, avoid involvement in other people's problems, spend money only on necessities and save all you can. And after all that . . . you can still break your neck in the bath tub and it will serve you right."[6] Her simple point is "Life is a risk."

We've probably all seen the insightful poem called *The Dilemma*, which reads:
>To laugh is to risk appearing a fool.
>To weep is to risk appearing sentimental.
>To reach out to another is to risk involvement.
>To expose feelings is to risk rejection.
>To place your dreams before the crowd is to risk ridicule.
>To love is to risk not being loved in return.
>To go forward in the face of overwhelming odds is to risk failure.

But risks must be taken because the great hazard in life is to risk nothing. The person who risks nothing does nothing, has nothing, is nothing. He may avoid suffering and sorrow (though that's debatable), but he cannot learn, feel, change, grow or love. Chained by his need for certainty, he is a slave. Only a person who risks is free.[7]

The truth is, if you're going to live at a higher level and truly walk by faith in Jesus Christ, you aren't always going to be able to play it safe. There's a built-in risk factor to living by faith. Luke 19:26, says, *"Risk your life and get more than you ever dreamed of; play it safe and you end up holding the bag."* So, I want to reflect a bit on five lessons I've learned on my faith journey that have helped me take a risk when God has asked me to step outside my comfort zone. You might want to think of these as Risk-taker Maxims to live by when you feel like playing it safe.

TRY AS WE MIGHT,

WE CANNOT

ELIMINATE RISK

FROM LIFE

Maxim #1:
If you want God's best, obey His request!

This is absolutely foundational to walking by faith. What God says goes - even when doing what He says may put you in hot water. Your job is to obey. It's God's job to take it from there. And whether or not things turn out the way you had hoped, just know this: If you obey, you'll be okay . . . no matter what. The shortest way to God's best is to obey His request!

In Daniel 3, Shadrach, Meshach and Abednego, are facing a real risk: Bow down or Burn! And their dilemma was, "Do we disobey God and save our skin, or do we obey and take the heat?" Daniel 3: 17-18 tells us their response: "We do not need to defend ourselves before you in this matter. If we are thrown into the blazing furnace, the God we serve is able to save us from it, and He will rescue us from your hand, O King." Notice the risk here because they don't know what God is going to do; they just know that if they obey God, they've done their job and the rest is up to Him.

So with resolute courage they take their stand: "But even if He does not (rescue us), we will not serve your gods or worship the image of gold you have set up." They were saying, "It doesn't matter what the stakes. Our faith is not open for compromise because we know that if we obey God's request, He'll give us His best! So, we'll take the heat and let God decide what's best from there." The rest is history: King Nebuchadnezzar got a front row seat that day to a display of God's power, as God sent an angel to deliver these three risk-takers from the fury of the flames.

Does that mean that God will always get us out of hot water by means of some miraculous deliverance? No! But I've come to understand that it's not my job to worry about what He's going to do. It's my job to do the right thing regardless and let Him decide the outcome. I just know that if I obey, I'll be okay, regardless. And we might add to this maxim as well, "When you obey His command, God does the unplanned!" You don't know what He's going to do or how, but you do know that when you obey, it's going to be okay. And if you've obeyed God, you've done your job. Now, you've made room for God to do His.

For instance, a young lady might think she'll lose her boyfriend if she doesn't give him what he wants, even though she knows she would be compromising her faith and God's standard if she were to give in to him. What should she do? Well, this maxim says it all: *"If you want God's best, obey His request!"*

Perhaps you're being asked to compromise your integrity at work and you fear that if you stand up to the boss, you'll be canned. What should you do? *"If you want God's best, obey His request!"*

You're at a drinking party and you know you shouldn't be there, but you're afraid that others will make fun of you if you refuse to drink, or better yet, leave. What should you do? *"If you want God's best, obey His request!"*

For me, I needed to ask forgiveness and be reconciled to a man that I feared would try to control what God had called me to do. What should I do? If I wanted God's best, I needed to obey His request!

I may not know what His best will turn out to be, but I know that obedience is the shortest way to it! So remember: *"If you want God's best, obey His request."*

Maxim #2:
When you follow God's lead, your plans succeed!

IT'S MY JOB TO DO THE RIGHT THING REGARDLESS AND LET HIM DECIDE THE OUTCOME

To be honest, even when you are following God's lead, it may not always look like you're succeeding. In reality, sometimes when you're following God's lead, it may look like you're experiencing the biggest failure of your life. But the important question always is, "Am I following God's lead?"

I have often faced my risks by claiming Proverbs 16:3, which says, *"Commit to the Lord whatever you do, and your plans will succeed."* And part of what it means to commit anything to the Lord is being able to say, "Okay Lord, I am yielding this totally to you. If you want me to go this direction, open the door. If you don't want me to go this direction, close the door. At any time that you want me to do something different than I am doing, just show me. But as I undertake what I believe you have called me to do, I'm going to work at it with all my heart believing that you will be working along with me." *When you follow God's lead, your plans succeed!*

With this maxim, the biggest question usually is: *How do I know what God's lead is where it is not clearly spelled out in the Bible?* When I packed up my family and all my belongings and headed to Peoria to start a new church in 1990, there was nothing in the Bible that told me specifically to do that. When you don't have a clear word from Scripture, you have the added risk of misreading what you think is a leading. So I wondered, "What if I moved to Peoria thinking I was following God's leading, only to discover that I was wrong?" This is why it's so important that we discern between a genuine call from God and what might simply be a foolish impulse on our part. Risk-taking itself is not enough. It must be accompanied by wisdom and discernment. So how do we discern God's leading?

RISK-TAKING ITSELF
IS NOT ENOUGH.
IT MUST BE
ACCOMPANIED BY
WISDOM AND
DISCERNMENT

The first way to discern a leading from God is to *look at the dreams in your heart.* What's captured your attention? Many times God's leading will come not as a dream you went looking for but as a dream that came looking for you. I still get goose bumps when I think of how God birthed a dream in my heart through a radio program back in 1988, while I was returning home from a vacation in Florida.

As Dr. James Dobson was interviewing a young pastor named Bill Hybels, everything in my heart was drawn like a magnet to the whole idea of building a church to reach the unchurched. Through my tears, I prayed a prayer in the car that day: "Oh God, if I could ever be a part of a church like that, that would be everything for me!" He puts a dream in your heart. That's one way He leads.

Second, *look at your gifts and talents,* because God will not usually call you to do something that He has not gifted you to do. Now that doesn't mean that you will necessarily feel up to the task. There will always be a huge challenge in anything God calls you to do that will make you feel a sense of shrinking back. But at the same time, He will equip you for the call He gives you.

In time, as you pray about that dream, *watch for the doors that open to you!* I didn't self-manufacture my dream of building a church for the unchurched. I didn't have it laid out on paper somewhere. The dream found me, and then God crafted both the timing and the place and presented the opportunity to me. I've found that when God wants you to walk through a door, you don't have to knock the door down. It will open to you.

GOD WILL NOT USUALLY CALL YOU TO DO SOMETHING THAT HE HAS NOT GIFTED YOU TO DO

Finally, *seek confirmation from the people around you.* Ask some trusted mentors and friends, "Does this seem like a fit for me? What's your sense?" God will give you confirmation because He really wants you to go forward in faith.

I remember when I finally decided that I was going to move to Peoria. I was an emotional wreck for a few days. So one evening I decided that I was going to stay up all night if I had to and ask God to help me become more certain in my spirit about His leading. I had pulled several magazines off my bookshelf that I had never read but which looked like they might offer me some help in my decision-making. An article in one of my *Leadership* magazines, entitled, "The Loneliest Choice of All" caught my attention. So I pulled the issue and said to myself, "Well, I can't imagine a more lonely decision than what this one feels like."

So after praying for a while that night, I turned to this article and was surprised to discover that the writer was a pastor discussing the agonizing decision of how to know when it's time to leave one church for another. At that point I was thinking, "Tell me everything you know. I'm all ears." Towards the end of the article, he says he called his mom one day to talk about it and she said to him, "I don't know what you're going to do, but I'm sure you'll do the right thing, *Cal*."

Now you need to know that growing up I hated the name "Cal" because I didn't know another person in the world who had that name. I've since found maybe two or three others. But it wasn't lost on me that when I was praying for confirmation, God led me to an article written by a man with the same name, who happened to be writing about the very decision I was now making. I try not to be too "nutty" about things like that, but it definitely got my attention.

IF YOU HAVE HIS LEADING, GO FOR IT AND LET GOD DEAL WITH THE SUCCESS

Then, another real interesting thing happened when I called my mom to tell her we were probably going to be moving (and you have to know my mom because she's always tried to stay out of the way and just be supportive of my decisions). I had never known her to have too much to say either way about my decisions. So I was literally blown away when she said, "Oh, I thought you'd probably start that church."

I asked, "Mom, what do you mean you thought I probably would?"

She said, "Well, when I first read about this new church starting in Peoria, I just thought it seemed like a good fit for you." It was as if God had given my mom a leading before He had even given it to me!

That just set me free to roll the dice and say, "Okay God! Even if I'm wrong, you know I believe you're leading me. I believe you've confirmed it so I'm diving in. And even though I don't know what's going to happen and I have no guarantee of success, I believe all the factors point to this being a leading from you!"

The bottom line is, if you have His leading, go for it and let God worry about the success. So remember: *"When you follow God's lead, your plans succeed!"*

Maxim #3:
Where God guides, He also provides!

If God tells you to do something, He will give you the energy, the talent, the ability, the people, the money, the space, the resources, the contacts, the network . . . whatever you need. But you've got to commit first. In my office, I keep a laminated card on which is this saying:

THE STORY OF NORTHWOODS COMMUNITY CHURCH HAS BEEN A STORY OF GOD GUIDING AND PROVIDING ALL ALONG

"Until I am committed, there is a hesitancy, a chance to draw back. But the moment I definitely commit myself, then God moves also, and a whole stream of events erupt. All manner of unforeseen incidents, meetings, persons and material assistance, which I could never have dreamed would come my way, begin to flow toward me the moment I make a commitment."[8]

That's because where God guides, He also provides. Philippians 4:19 says, "My God will fully supply whatever you need according to His glorious riches in Christ Jesus." Not only in my personal life, but also as a church leader, I have witnessed this maxim over and over again. Where God has guided, He has always provided.

The story of Northwoods Community Church has been a

story of God guiding and providing all along. Let me just recount for you a few of the wonderful things God has done for our church along the way. Back in 1991, when we began looking for land on which to build one day, we were focused on a piece just a mile up the road from where we ultimately ended up building. The going price was $20,000 an acre for 40 acres and only 30 of those acres were usable. A little bit of quick math told us that we needed to come up with $800,000. That sum told us right there and then, "God, if we're going to have the land we will one day need for this ministry, it's going to have to be something you miraculously bring about."

Not long thereafter, a member of our small leadership team presented us with the possibility of buying a different 40-acre parcel of land. Some of us weren't convinced it was as good of a location as the original piece, because it was a bit off the beaten path at that time. There was nothing near it but cornfields. But it had a couple of things going for it - the cost was $135,000 instead of $800,000 and all 40 acres were usable.

WE DON'T KNOW HOW AND WHEN HE'S GOING TO PROVIDE, AND THAT CAN MAKE FOR SOME INTERESTING MOMENTS WHILE WE'RE WAITING

The only problem was, the owner wanted us to come up with the money in just a matter of weeks. So, I went before our people and asked, "Should we go for it? Will you help us go for it?" Their answer was a unanimous "yes", even though that $135,000 price tag was a real stretch for us at that time. However, people gave generously and when it came time to close, the Lord brought across my path a man who was interested in helping us secure that land. He came to my office one day and basically said, "Whatever it will take to get it done, let me know."

On the day of our closing, we were $15,000 short. So, I called up this recent acquaintance and told him, "We still need

$15,000." And unbelievably, he wired us the final $15,000 at the 11th hour and 59th minute on the day we were to close. That was truly a miraculous moment in the life of our young church, proving once again that where God guides, He also provides! We just don't know how and when He's going to provide, and that can make for some interesting moments while we're waiting.

In May of 1993, the timing wasn't quite right yet to build a facility on our land. So we decided to purchase an interim facility, in the form of an abandoned truck dock, and sink $300,000 into fixing it up. At that point, there was some legitimate concern expressed that not only would we probably never get our money out of it, but also we were going to have a very difficult time selling the building because it was a limited use facility. But God was getting ready to prove to us again that where He guides, He also provides.

I WOULD RATHER DO SOMETHING STUPID BECAUSE I BELIEVED GOD WANTED ME TO, THAN TO DO NOTHING AT ALL BECAUSE I DIDN'T HAVE ENOUGH FAITH TO RISK ANYTHING FOR THE LORD

Before I finish the rest of this story, I want you to be clear about something. When you're walking by faith, sometimes you will feel like you are simultaneously standing on the verge of either the most wonderful miracle you have ever witnessed or the stupidest decision you've ever made. You can't get away from that tension. So I have decided that when faced with that tension in my life, I would rather do something stupid because I believed God wanted me to, than to do nothing at all because I didn't have enough faith to risk anything for the Lord. Back to the story...

In August of 1997, when it came time for us to move out of the truck dock and build a church on our land, not only did the facility sell very quickly, but we actually entertained notions of turning down the first buyer since there were several others who wanted it (we thought we could possibly get a better deal with a little competition). But, so much for the original concern that no one would want a limited use facility.

And what kind of deal did we get in the resale? We had hoped at the bare minimum to at least cover the $380,000 mortgage we had left to pay on the building. We figured we'd probably do a bit better than that, but we also figured we'd lose quite a bit of the money we had invested in fixing up the place. Bottom line, we actually got back every dollar we ever invested in the truck dock. So much for the original concern that we'd never get our money out of it!

Perhaps some challenge is calling for a bit of risk-taking in your life right now. I want to encourage you to step forward with courage and boldness if you believe God is guiding you. And you will discover, as I have over and over again, *"Where God guides, He also provides!"*

Maxim #4:
What you invest will come back blessed!

I have been amazed at God's math over and over again. I can't explain it, but many of you have discovered as well that you can't out give God. In God's work, you never lose what you invest. Instead, you receive it back blessed. Luke 6:38 says, "Give and it will be given to you. A good measure, pressed down, shaken together and running over, will be poured into your lap. For with the measure you use, it will be measured to you." Simply put: *What you invest will come back blessed!*

This is why I never concerned myself with what happened to the stock market in the weeks following the September 11th attack on America. Those of us who were investing for the future took some hits. And maybe we were tempted to worry and fret over it. As I was praying about it one day, God gave me a word in my spirit that if I would continue to focus on generous investment in His cause, He would take care of my other investments. I sensed Him saying to me, "Cal, when have I ever allowed you to out give me! You stay focused on investing in my cause, and I'll take care of your other causes." And it struck me, "What if the return I receive on my other investments is proportional to the generosity with which I've invested in God's causes?" Interesting thought!

But that's what Jesus said: "The measure you use, is the measure I'll bless." In other words, if you give to Him in a one-cup measure, He fills up that one cup, packs it down and sends it back. You get one cup, packed down and overflowing. If you give it to Him in a one-quart measure, you get one quart back, packed down and overflowing! The measure you use is the measure He blesses. But regardless of the measure, what you give to God, He multiplies.

IN GOD'S WORK, YOU NEVER LOSE WHAT YOU INVEST. INSTEAD, YOU RECEIVE IT BACK BLESSED

Anyone who is willing to step out in faith and invest in God's cause will discover the truth of this maxim. In fact, I have kept a lot of letters over the years that people have sent to me, testifying to the truth of God's blessing. During a stewardship campaign at our church in 1999, one couple that made a commitment, which would require both faith and sacrifice, wrote to me a few months later. Their letter read in part:

Dear Cal,

"We have been hesitant to share our story with you for no other reason than the privacy of our giving relationship with God. But since He won't seem to relieve us of the prodding to tell you of our experience, it must be something you need to know.

"When contemplating what to do in giving toward the building program, beyond our tithes and offerings, we had prayed independent of the other and both arrived at the same amount . . . $10,000 over the three years. But this seemed achievable without much sacrifice. So we repeated the process, leading to a challenging $15,000, realizing a little 'tightening of the belt' would be required. That meant cutting the cable TV from basic programming of $32/month to 'starvation' programming of $11/month. (I guess we could go on a TV fast, but I felt that a few morsels of programming wouldn't hurt). I'm going to stay out of my car hobby for at least the duration of the campaign, saving the license, insurance costs, etc. and applying it toward our pledge. Like you and your wife, we decided that our 12 year-old, 190,000 mile car would have to last another three years and maybe up to 250,000 miles. I think you get the picture. THEN, just when we felt up to the challenge, God prompted us to double the commitment to $30,000. We didn't know where the money would come from, but we had the assurance it would somehow be there, even if it meant selling off some assets to meet the pledge.

YOU DON'T HAVE TO WONDER WHETHER YOUR TIME, TALENT AND TREASURE INVESTED IN GOD'S CAUSE GOES UNNOTICED

"So what has God done? Within a matter of weeks after making our pledge, God saw fit to provide both my wife and me, collectively, with unexpected salary increases to cover our 'leap of faith' pledge and increase our giving to the general funding needs of the church. The increase is a lot, but it's the timing of it that we find more incredible, which further evidences God's hand in it. Any raises we have received in the past have always occurred on our respective employment anniversary, but not in this case.

"You know, Cal, the extension of this, simply stated, means more giving capacity, which is exactly what we are doing. Yes, God does do miraculous things, and Yes, His bucket is bigger than ours, and Yes, sacrifice allows God to demonstrate His promises. **Our God is an Awesome God!**"

Amazing, isn't it? You don't have to wonder whether your time, talent and treasure invested in God's cause goes unnoticed. Mark 10:29-30 says, "You won't regret it. No one who has sacrificed his home, spouse, brothers, sisters, parents, children - whatever - will lose out. It'll all come back, multiplied many times over in your lifetime and then the bonus of eternal life." I've taken a lot of risks in this area of my life and I can tell you: *What you invest will come back blessed!*

We turn now to one final maxim that I like to call, "God's safety net."

Maxim #5:
When your hopes go unmet, God's not done yet!

There are going to be some risks you take that don't turn out the way you had hoped they would. Sometimes in following God, you're going to make a mistake. Sometimes you're going to get hurt. Sometimes your prayers are going to go unanswered. Sometimes you're going to feel like God has not rewarded your step of faith. Sometimes you're going to obey God and feel like you got burned instead of delivered from the fire.

As I have followed Christ over the years, I've suffered a lot of setbacks. I've cried a lot of tears. I've known my share of setbacks and disappointments. Over the years, some of my hopes have gone unmet. But I always remind myself, "God's not done yet!"

Perhaps you've been praying for a specific situation and nothing's changed. Maybe you've been praying for a wayward son or daughter and they're as wayward now as the day you started praying. Perhaps you've been praying for an unsaved family member or friend for a long time and today it seems that they're as far from Christ as they've ever been. You're perhaps tempted to wonder whether your prayers are doing any good because your hopes have gone unmet. But remember, God's not done yet! And He's not done with your life yet. Philippians 1:6 says you can be confident "that He who began a good work in you will carry it on to completion until the day of Christ Jesus."

You may be walking through a valley where it feels like your prayers, your needs, your hopes and your dreams have gone unmet. You need to know today, God's not done yet! You might be battling with problems in your life or an addiction that you can't break and your hopes have gone unmet. God's not done yet! Perhaps you're going through a season where you feel like you risked it all and it's turned into the biggest disaster of your life, and your hopes have gone unmet. Let me remind you: God's not done yet!

There was a Friday and a Saturday, 2,000 years ago, when the disciples were locked in a room, mourning the loss of their best friend, and feeling a bit foolish for having risked that maybe this Jesus was the Christ. Yet now He was dead. Their hopes had gone unmet . . . but God wasn't done yet! He was just waiting until Sunday!!!

In June of 2001, I buried my sister after taking the risk for two years that if I believed and prayed in faith, she might be healed. But she died . . . and my hopes went unmet, but God's not done yet! My sister is alive with Jesus today and is enjoying life at a much higher level than she has ever known. And one day, if we walk by faith, we too will come to that moment when it's our time to go. Those who love us will be praying for God to give us some extra years, and their hopes will go unmet. But, praise God, He won't be done yet!

When you take a risk for God, and pin your trust in Him, you can't lose. And even when you feel like you have lost, remind yourself: *"When your hopes go unmet, God's not done yet!"*

The fact is that you can't avoid risk! Risk is inherent to life. In fact, taking risks is the only way to live. Otherwise, we become like the guy I read about in this poem:

> *There once lived a man who never risked,*
> *he never chanced, he never tried;*
> *He never cared, he never loved,*
> *he never laughed, he never cried.*
> *And then one day when he passed away,*
> *his insurance was denied.*
> *They said since he'd never really lived,*
> *he'd never really died!*[9]

WHEN YOU TAKE A RISK FOR GOD, AND PIN YOUR TRUST IN HIM, YOU CAN'T LOSE

If you're going to really live, and live by faith, you're going to have to face the risk factor. You can't avoid that. But what you can do when facing a risk is bet on these risk-taker maxims, and you'll find, as I have, that God always comes through.

> *Oh God, summon me to take the risk, and give me courage to embrace the risk of faith, knowing that playing it safe has never satisfied my soul. I want to live out on the edge with you. I want to witness your mighty acts in my life. I want to live like I believe that you really will come through for me when I am faced with a fiery test of faith. Help me to remember that you have given me the safety net of these faith maxims, and that in the end, I can't lose if I trust you by faith! In Jesus name, Amen.*

Sometimes, when we are forced to endure difficult times, our faith will be challenged and tested. It's then that we need a tenacious faith . . . a faith that will go the distance. We'll talk about how to develop a faith like that in the next chapter.

CHAPTER SEVEN

*"God does every thing just right and on time,
but people can never completely
understand what He's doing."*

ECCLESIASTES 3:11

BUILDING A TENACIOUS FAITH

I've discovered in life that there are some things perseverance and persistence can get you that nothing else can. In fact, it's one of the great lessons of life. A three-year-old boy had that all figured out when he went with his mom to the grocery store. Before they entered, she gave him some final instructions: "Now you're not going to get any chocolate chip cookies, so don't even ask." She put him in the child's seat and off they went up and down the aisles.

He was doing just fine until they came to the cookie section. Seeing the chocolate chip cookies, he said, "Mom, can I have some chocolate chip cookies?" She was a bit taken back at his audacity to even ask since she had laid down the ground rules before coming into the store. So she said, "I told you not even to ask. You're not getting any cookies, no matter what!"

They continued down the aisles, but in their search for certain items she had to back track and ended up in the cookie aisle again. Bad move!! Seeing the cookies, the little guy asks again, "Mom, can I please have some chocolate chip cookies?" She says even more firmly than before, "I've already told you two times that you are not getting any chocolate chip cookies. Now sit still and be quiet."

Finally, they arrived at the checkout. The little boy sensed the end was in sight - that this might be his last chance. He stood up on the seat and shouted in his loudest voice, "In the name of Jesus, may I have some chocolate chip cookies?" Everyone in the checkout lanes laughed and applauded. And guess what? That conniving little tyke got his cookies. The other shoppers, moved by his daring, pooled their resources and the little guy left the store with 23 boxes of chocolate chip cookies! Now, how's that for being told you aren't going to get any cookies? Sometimes perseverance and persistence will get you what nothing else can.

SOMETIMES PERSEVERANCE AND PERSISTENCE WILL GET YOU WHAT NOTHING ELSE CAN

You are probably familiar with the life story of one of the great leaders of our country:

He was born into poverty. When he was seven-years-old, his family was forced out of their home on a legal technicality and he had to work to help support the family.

At age nine, his mother died.

At 22, he lost his job as a store clerk. He wanted to go to law school, but his education wasn't good enough.

That same year, he ran for the state legislature and lost.

At 23, he went into debt to become a partner in a small store. By the end of the year, he was bankrupt. He spent the next 17 years of his life paying off his debt.

At 24, he ran for the state legislature and won.

At 26 and engaged to be married, his fiancée died.

At 27, he had a nervous breakdown and was in bed for six months.

At 29, he sought to become speaker of the state legislature and lost.

At 31, he attempted to become elector and lost.

At 34, he ran for Congress and lost.

At 37, on his third try, he was elected to Congress.

At 39, he ran for re-election to Congress and lost.

At 40, he sought the job of land officer in his home state and was rejected.

At 41, his four-year old son died.

At 45, he ran for the Senate of the United States and lost.

At 47, he sought his party's Vice Presidential nomination and got fewer than 100 votes.

At 49, he ran for the Senate again, and lost.

At 51, he was elected president of the United States.

Some people just get all the breaks, don't they? Of course, I'm referring to Abraham Lincoln, a man many consider to be the greatest leader our country has ever had known.

The truth is, whether it's getting that bag of chocolate chip cookies you long for or overcoming setback after setback in life to finally realize your dream, there are some things that only persistence and perseverance can get you that nothing else can. And nowhere is that more true than living a life of faith and pursuing God's purposes for your life.

That being the case, how do we build a persevering, persistent, tenacious faith that will hold on to Jesus Christ through thick and thin; a faith that knows how to pray and believe God for an answer; a faith that knows how to hang tough when the answer is slow in coming; and a faith that continues to trust God even in the worst of times? Why is such faith so important?

As you go through life, there are going to be times when you have to persist in faith without seeing the answer. There are going to be times when your dream doesn't seem worth pursuing anymore. There are going to be times when you're in God's waiting room. God's waiting room refers to those times when something you need is completely out of your control and you have to wait on God for an answer to prayer, a miracle, a change in a situation.

The Bible says in Ecclesiastes 3:11: "God does everything just right and on time, but people can never completely understand what He's doing." And we've probably all been there at one time or another. We've wondered, "God, what are you doing? Why aren't you answering my prayers? Why aren't you honoring my faith? Why aren't you coming through for me like you said you would?"

A man in the Bible, named Abraham, was certainly familiar with those sentiments. Rick Warren, the pastor of Saddleback Church in California, has pointed out, from Abraham's life, six phases of faith that God often takes us through, which require tremendous persistence and perseverance.[1]

> AS YOU GO THROUGH LIFE, THERE ARE GOING TO BE TIMES WHEN YOU HAVE TO PERSIST IN FAITH WITHOUT SEEING THE ANSWER

Phase I:
The Dream Phase

This is where God puts a dream, an idea, an ambition, and a goal into your heart. You can see it in your mind's eye. You know what your preferred future is. The dream has captured you.

In Genesis 12:1-3, Abram was just minding his business one day when God says, "Abram, I want you to leave here and go to the place I will show you because I am going to make you into a great nation." Abram doesn't know how God's going to do it, because he doesn't have any children and his wife is barren. Nonetheless, God says, "I'm going to bless you and give you a son." He's 75-years-old when that dream comes to Him. That's all he knows. He has a dream and some instructions.

Phase 2:
The Decision Phase

Now Abram has to decide whether or not he is going to act upon the dream God has given him. Likewise, there comes a time for all of us when, by faith, after we've done our homework and we've prayed about the dream and sought God's direction and turned it completely over to Him, that we step out and make a decision to pursue it.

This is where the risk factor we talked about in the last chapter comes into play. The Bible tells us in Genesis 12:4, "So Abram left, as the Lord had told him." Hebrews 11, the great faith chapter of the Bible says, "By faith, Abraham, when called to go to a place he would later receive as his inheritance, obeyed and went, even though he did not know where he was going." I love that phrase: *"Even though he did not know where he was going."* All he knew was that he was following God. That was enough! And there will be times when following God has to be enough for us.

That's about all I knew when I decided to become the pastor of Northwoods Community Church. I want to tell you that from a purely human standpoint, there is no logical explanation for why God has blessed Northwoods as much as He has. I had no experience in leading a new church plant when I arrived. As for building a church to reach the unchurched, you'd think that I would have studied everything there was to know about that for five years, and then perhaps spent another year training the core group. Not a chance! I wasn't smart enough to know that's how you plant a church. I had one 30-minute section of a radio program under my belt at the time.

GOD PUTS A DREAM, AN IDEA, AN AMBITION, AND A GOAL INTO YOUR HEART

I found out several months later that the recommended start-up plan for a church like ours was to have budget money raised and at least two or three other staff people with you at the start, plus a core group that thoroughly understood the mission, vision and strategy. I didn't even know what mission, vision and strategy were. I was thinking, "Set up the chairs and let's have church!"

I was flying by the seat of my pants. Do I normally recommend that as the way to do things? No! It's always better if you know in advance a little about what you're doing. But if God tells you it's time to go, you'd better go when He says 'go'. He had called us to do this, and I think right from the start He wanted to make sure we understood that He wasn't blessing it because of how smart we were. He was blessing our faith and our obedience.

THERE WILL BE TIMES WHEN FOLLOWING GOD HAS TO BE ENOUGH FOR US

For some of you, the tendency at the Decision Phase is going to be to wait until you're convinced you know everything you need to know. The only problem is that while you're trying to figure it all out and eliminate every last ounce of risk, the opportunity is passing you by.

God wants you to obey now and you're saying, "I've got to do a little more homework to be sure." And you've been doing your homework for five years! Do your homework but understand that you can never do enough to remove all the risk from your decision. There is always a faith risk in every decision we have to make - whether it's buying a car, deciding to get married, changing jobs or anything else you can name. You can't get away from risk.

No matter how much homework you do, any decision you need to make is still going to have a 25-30% chance of failure, because you can never bump the certainty factor above 70-75%. So there's always a window, where having done all the homework you can, you must step out in faith based upon what you do know and trusting God with what you don't know. That's the Decision Phase. But then we encounter turbulence.

Phase 3:
The Delay Phase

A dream is never fulfilled instantly. There is always a time gap between when God gives you an idea of what He wants to do with your life and when He actually fulfills it. And that gap is designed with your growth in mind. God has to prepare you today to receive what He wants to give you tomorrow. Rarely are we fully prepared at the moment He puts His dream in our hearts. So, in between the dream and the fulfillment there is always a waiting period.

In the Delay Phase, things get really tough and your faith is tested. God had given Abram a promise when he was 75-years-old. That's how old Abram was when he made a decision to stake his life on that promise and leave his home. But in Genesis 16:1, Abram is now 86-years-old and it has been 11 years since God first gave him the promise of a son. We read, "But Sarah still had not borne any children." Major delay! This is where doubts begin to play with your mind. You begin to think things like, "Maybe I screwed up. Maybe I didn't really hear God correctly. It was probably just wishful thinking on my part." But if the Delay Phase is tough, sometimes we go from major delay to major difficulty!

YOU MUST STEP OUT BASED UPON WHAT YOU DO KNOW AND TRUSTING GOD WITH WHAT YOU DON'T KNOW

Phase 4:
The Difficulty Phase

God not only lets you wait for a while, but during your wait He lets you have some problems. Isn't that fun? So you go through the stage of difficulty where things go from bad to really bad to worse to impossible. Abram thought he'd waited a while when he was 86 and didn't have a son. What do you suppose he was thinking at the age of 99, a whopping 24 years later, when he still did not have a son? He's 99 and his wife, Sarah, is 89.

GOD HAS TO

PREPARE YOU TODAY

TO RECEIVE WHAT

HE WANTS TO GIVE

YOU TOMORROW

They're not spring chickens anymore. And then God says, "It's going to happen next year." The Bible says that Abram was wrestling with the promise now as he asked in Genesis 17:17, "How can a son be born to a man who is a hundred years old?" Even he was laughing at the absurdity of it all. Abram was thinking, "God, this is going to be really difficult."

What's worse is that God changed Abram's name. Originally, his name was Abram, which means, "exalted father," and God changed his name to Abraham, which means, "Father of a great nation." And that's before he even had a son!

Imagine Abraham walking into the local diner where the waitress says, "What's your name?"

"Father of a great nation."

"Oh? How many kids do you have?"

"None . . . yet!"

"By the way, how old are you?"

"I'm 99."

You understand? That's kind of embarrassing.

That's what it was like for Abraham and that's what it will be like for us sometimes. We will have the witness inside our heart of what God is going to do before it happens, but we can't prove it to anyone else because as Hebrews 11:1 says, "Faith is the substance of things hoped for, the evidence of things not seen." If we're trusting God for things that are only hoped for and not seen, then people are going to think we're crazy at times because we have no empirical evidence to convince them otherwise.

I've been there before and it hurts when you believe you're simply doing what God wants you to do and some of the people around you think you're losing your mind. You begin to wonder if you may be, because you can't prove to them that what you believe is going to happen is really going to happen. When you're walking by faith, time is really the only thing that can verify your faith.

While you might think the Difficulty Phase would be the hardest, there's one more phase that's tough.

Phase 5:
The Dead-end Phase

At a dead-end, God allows your dream to be crushed. Abraham, when he was 100-years-old, finally got his son. God had fulfilled His promise to Abraham. And life couldn't have been better for Abraham until a few years later when God said, "Abraham! I want you to take Isaac up the mountain and sacrifice him."

And I imagine Abraham thought, "Say what? God, that doesn't make sense. You said you wanted to give me a son and that through him you would make me into a great nation. Now you're telling me to sacrifice my son. I don't get it!"

How do you know when you're at a dead-end? You feel hopeless. Maybe you are at a dead-end in your marriage right now. Maybe you are at a dead-end with respect to the prospects for marriage. Maybe you are at a dead-end in your budget. Maybe it is your career, a key relationship, or your relationship with your parents. Maybe you are at a physical dead-end and your health is falling apart. When you're at this stage, you start to doubt God's wisdom and love and you say things like, "Why is this happening to me?"

When you get to a dead-end, Congratulations! God has you about where He wants you. At this stage, you realize that if the dream is going to be fulfilled, He's going to have to do it.

WHEN YOU'RE WALKING BY FAITH, TIME IS REALLY THE ONLY THING THAT CAN VERIFY YOUR FAITH

Hebrews 11:19 says Abraham reasoned that God could raise the dead, so he figured, "Hey, he raised Isaac from a dead womb in the first place. I guess He can do it again." But here you just resign yourself into God's hands and say, "God, if you want it to happen, you're going to have to do it." All you can do at a dead-end is trust Him! That's when God says, "Now, I've got you where I want you!" And, you're ready for the final phase.

Phase 6:
The Deliverance Phase

The greater the dead-end and the more hopeless the situation, the greater the deliverance is going to be. You'll say, "Wow! Only God could have done that." Just like Abraham did when, at the age of 100, his barren wife, then 90, gives birth to a son. And they laughed so hard at the absurdity of it all that they actually named their son "Laughter," which is the Hebrew translation of Isaac. That's something else that happens at the stage of deliverance. The greater the dead-end, the deeper the belly laugh when God works it out. You just shake your head in amazement.

If you're a follower of Jesus, God is going to take you through these six phases of faith many, many times in life. Over and over again you'll go from dream to decision to delay to difficulty to dead-end to deliverance. Then He'll do it again and then He'll do it again for the purpose of growing and stretching your faith. Therefore, it's important that you understand what's going on when you're in the Delay, Difficulty or Dead-end phase.

It's not time to throw in the towel. It's time to get tenacious and hang on to God's promises - to hang on to the dream He has put in your heart. You see, a persistent and persevering faith will many times bring you what nothing else can. This is why the Bible says in Hebrews 10:35-36, to some believers who were really going through difficult times, "So do not throw away your confidence; it will be richly rewarded. You need to persevere so that when you have done the will of God, you will receive what He has promised."

THE GREATER THE DEAD-END, THE DEEPER THE BELLY LAUGH WHEN GOD WORKS IT OUT

Hebrews 11 makes it clear that the ultimate realization of what God has promised will only happen when we get to heaven. Yes, God fulfills some of our dreams here as a preview of what is to come. But we also experience the disappointment of unfulfilled dreams that will ultimately be fulfilled in heaven. That requires us to persevere in faith, even when we haven't gotten what we were promised. So how do we develop a persevering faith that will go the distance?

Draw Encouragement from Your Balcony People!

Balcony people refer to those who are in the stands cheering for you. Of course, with only a few slight changes to "balcony", you end up with "baloney." Every one of us needs to know the difference between "balcony people" and "baloney people." Balcony people cheer for you. Baloney people jeer at you. Balcony people light the fire of your passion. Baloney people fight the fire of your passion. Balcony people pray for you. Baloney people prey on you. Balcony people are people-builders. Baloney people are people-wilters. You've got to know the difference and, in pursuing the dream God has for you, make sure to surround yourself with the right people.

I remember one guy who had a dream to be a speaker. He said, "My friends didn't think I could be a good speaker so I did something about it. I went out and found some new friends."

We all need real, live balcony people. But Hebrews 12:1 draws our attention to another set of balcony people who are cheering for us as we seek to follow Jesus Christ and live by faith. In Hebrews 11, the Hall-of-Faith chapter in the Bible, we are introduced to a line-up of people who have gone before us and have run the race of faith. Abel, Enoch, Noah, Abraham, Isaac, Jacob, Joseph, Moses, Rahab, Gideon, Barak, Samson, David, Samuel . . . these great giants of the faith have all made it to the finish line. Now they're in the stands cheering for us.

Hebrews 12:1 says, "Therefore, since we are surrounded by such a great cloud of witnesses . . ." This great cloud of witnesses is comprised of these past giants of the faith. They're up in the grandstands cheering us on and saying, "Come on, hang in there no matter what! God's not asking you to go through anything He hasn't asked us to go through. We made it and so can you."

When I think of that great cloud of witnesses, I get a picture of my son Jonathon a couple of years ago at one of his seventh grade track meets. His main event was the mile run. At one of the track meets early in the year, all the kids were sitting up in the stands and each time Jonathon came down the stretch in front of the stands, they'd break into a chant, "Johnny, Johnny, Johnny." And those kids had no idea what they were doing for him at that moment. He told my wife later that night, "Mom, did you hear them? They were cheering for me!"

What about you? Do you hear them? They're cheering for you! If you're in a very difficult phase right now and you feel hopeless, if you've been disappointed by the latest medical news, if you've been praying for a healing that hasn't come, if you've been praying for a situation that's only gotten worse instead of better, you need to know there is a whole grandstand full of people today cheering for you and saying, "Don't give up! Stay the course, no matter how difficult it gets. You will be so glad you did, because there's a victory stand coming one day in heaven. And whether or not you see the fulfillment of every dream in this life, that's the victory stand you want to be on one day. So don't give up!"

All your balcony people have been there. They know you can do it and they're calling your name. So draw encouragement from them.

GOD FULFILLS SOME OF OUR DREAMS HERE AS A PREVIEW OF WHAT IS TO COME

Offload Any Hindrances to Your Faith!

Hebrews 12:1 says, "Let us throw off everything that hinders." A few years ago, I did a very foolish thing: I trained for and ran a marathon. As difficult as that was, I want you to know that I didn't make it more difficult by wearing ankle weights and combat boots.

In fact, about six months after I had run my marathon, I actually dropped 15 pounds and the difference was amazing. Only then did I realize how much that extra weight had been hindering me and slowing me down. Likewise, we need to ask: Are there hindrances in my life that are acting like extra weight and keeping me from God's purposes for me?

You may have friendships that are keeping you from God's

best. You know those friendships aren't helping you grow in your faith, but you're afraid to move on. Sometimes you have to say goodbye to people who are only slowing you down. In other words, you have to give up to go up! Sometimes you have to throw off the dead weight of routines that are hindering you. You give up a bit of late night television so you can do some morning Bible study. You have to give up to go up. Perhaps you have some old habits that are slowing you down in your faith journey. You have to give up to go up! Where in your life are there hindrances to your life of faith? If you're going to run with perseverance, offload the things that slow you down.

YOU NEED TO KNOW THERE IS A WHOLE GRANDSTAND FULL OF PEOPLE TODAY CHEERING FOR YOU AND SAYING, "DON'T GIVE UP!"

Guard Your Life Against Faith-Robbing Entanglements!

Hebrews 12:1 encourages us to throw off not only everything that hinders, but also the "sin that so easily entangles." I find that sin comes pretty easily and naturally to me if I don't guard my life against it. I can say things and do things and think things that are totally contrary to what God wants for me. So I have to be diligent about renewing my mind and not allowing myself to dabble with those things that can entangle me.

The danger here is that when we are engaged in something God says we shouldn't be entangled in, it erodes the confidence of our faith. I have known times in my life when I wanted to ask God for something, but I had no confidence in asking Him for it because I knew I was not living like I should be. Sin was compromising my confidence. So be ruthless in guarding your life against those kinds of entanglements.

If you can't use the computer without viewing moral filth, it'd be better for you to get rid of your computer. If you can't have a drink without getting sloshed, it'd be better to nix the drink. If going into a bar makes you vulnerable to relational entanglements, it'd be better to stay out of the bar. Some of this is common sense.

It's like the guy who went to his doctor and said, "Doc, I broke my arm in two places. What should I do?" The doctor said, "Stay out of those places." If your goal is to build a faith that will go the distance, there are some places you might have to stay out of. Don't get entangled!

Focus on the Payoff Instead of the Pain!

When I was in high school, I hated practicing basketball all summer long in the loneliness of my smelly basketball court, with only a barn full of steers staring at me. What I learned to do though, which I didn't know was a Biblical principle at the time, was to hold in my head the image of what it would feel like the next winter to be playing before a packed gym and how good it would feel then if I put in the time now. I learned to focus on the payoff instead of the pain and that served as a motivator in my life. That's what we have to learn to do on our faith journey as well.

SOMETIMES YOU HAVE TO SAY GOODBYE TO PEOPLE WHO ARE ONLY SLOWING YOU DOWN

When you go through a period of time where you wonder if living by faith is worth it, when there is delay and difficulty and dead-end, you have to reconnect with the future God has called you to and say, "That's what I'm after. Thus, I am not going to quit." With that picture fixed firmly in your mind, you say, "I'm going to live consistently right now with what I know the future is going to be."

That's how Jesus endured the cross. He didn't focus on the pain. Oh, He felt it, but Hebrews 12:2 says, "...who for the joy set before him endured the cross." Do you see? Jesus had a picture in His mind of what it was going to be like on the other side of that cross and through faith, He persevered. And because He did, He opened heaven to all of us who have chosen to put our faith in Him. When the going gets tough, mentally and emotionally connect with the payoff instead of the pain and you will find the will to persevere.

Fix Your Eyes on Jesus!

FIX YOUR EYES ON

JESUS INSTEAD OF ON

THE FUTILITY OF YOUR

UNFULFILLED DREAM

Hebrews 12:2 enjoins us, "Let us fix our eyes on Jesus, the author and perfecter of our faith…" When you're called to endure, and you wonder why God is allowing you to undergo what you're going through, and you need a faith for hanging on, fix your eyes on Jesus instead of on the futility of your unfulfilled dream. Through focusing on Him, you will find the strength and power to endure.

God has not promised to take away all of your pain . . . yet! He has not promised that all of your loved ones are going to live as long as you want them to live. God has not promised that you will not have difficulties, that you will not have dead-ends, never have any delays. He has not promised to take away all your pain. He has promised to give you everything you need to handle the delays, the difficulties and the dead-ends, if you keep your eyes on Him. And He has promised that one day He will deliver you to heaven where there is no sorrow or suffering or sadness or pain.

That takes a faith that will go the distance and that's the kind of faith He is committed to developing in you. So if you're in the Delay Phase, the Difficulty Phase or the Dead-end Phase, seek God for a breakthrough with all the faith you can muster. But regardless of if or when the breakthrough comes, cling to Him with tenacious faith.

> *Lord, I pray that you'll develop within me a faith that will go the distance. Help me to persevere whenever I face difficult faith challenges, knowing that my reward is up ahead in heaven. Help me to run with perseverance the race marked out for me and to keep my eyes fixed on you until I reach the finish line. In Jesus name, Amen.*

The greatest lessons I have ever learned in faith have pertained to my finances. Generous giving, even when you're not sure how God is going to provide, opens the way for God to pour out His provisions in your life. In fact, there's probably nothing that reveals the strength of our faith quite like how we're allowing faith to impact our finances. We'll talk about that challenge in the next chapter.

CHAPTER EIGHT

"For the eyes of the Lord range throughout the earth to strengthen those whose hearts are fully committed to Him."

2 CHRONICLES 16:9

APPLYING FAITH TO YOUR FINANCES

As I look back over my life, it is abundantly clear that the greatest times of growth in my relationship with God have all come through challenges which really stretched and deepened my faith. God has often taken me to places where faith in Him was all I had. And through these experiences, He has taught me that faith in Him is all I'll ever need.

My greatest lessons in preparation for a life of ministry have not come from my courses of study and theological books. Rather, they've come out of having to trust God with a need and then seeing Him come through time and time and time again. I can truthfully tell you that I wouldn't trade those lessons for anything in the world, because it was out of these special times of need that I came to know God in a new way and learned to understand that He really could meet my needs in a very personal way.

So many times those faith challenges have centered on financial issues in my life. I believe that's just the way it is because our financial resources, like nothing else, represent a form of security to us. Subtly, and often without our being even remotely aware, these resources can actually seek to erode our trust in God, and to place it instead in our bank accounts or checkbooks. And we only begin to realize how strong that attachment to our resources is when God challenges us to give some of them up. That's why speaking on the topic of financial stewardship and sacrificial giving tends not to be a favorite for most pastors. It's a topic that strikes at our sense of security.

Come to think of it, I can't ever remember anyone in my church coming up to me and saying, "Cal, when are you going to do a series on giving. I just want to learn how to be a better giver!"

And yet I have often sensed the ironic twist in my own life that it's through the very issue of honoring God in my giving that I have most often seen His miraculous provision at work. Why wouldn't I want people to understand what they need to know on this topic?

IT WAS OUT OF THESE SPECIAL TIMES OF NEED THAT I CAME TO KNOW GOD IN A NEW WAY

Over and over again, God has shown me that if I put Him first and honor Him with the first fruits of all my income, He will personally take care of seeing that my needs are met in one way or another. If there's anything I would love for you to experience, it's precisely this faith lesson: When, through faith in God, you give to Him what you feel you can't afford to live without, you invariably end up with more than enough. But when through fear and unbelief you keep for yourself that which should be given, you never have enough. Many times in my faith journey, God has reinforced that lesson in my life.

At a very young age, I learned that basic obedience to God in my finances meant giving Him at least one tenth of everything I earned. Whether mowing lawns, bailing hay, or cleaning the restaurant, I was always faithful to God in that simple act of obedience. But because of my high school schedule, I did not have a regular job outside of cleaning a restaurant a couple times a week. And this part-time endeavor essentially provided me gas and lunch money each week.

So it may not seem like a big thing to you the day I learned that I needed an extra $7.50 to send in my SAT scores. I was still dragging my feet about going to college and wanted to be absolutely sure that this was God's plan for me. I remember praying, "Lord, any idea where I can come up with an extra $7.50 real quick?"

It wasn't lost on me that very day when the guidance counselor came up to me and said, "Cal, I had no idea that we were going to get paid for that little workshop you helped me with last weekend. But we received $30 and the only fair way I know to divvy it up is to divide it among the four of us who helped out." (I'll let you do the math)

LORD, ANY IDEA WHERE I CAN COME UP WITH AN EXTRA $7.50 REAL QUICK?

It may not seem like much to you, but it was in "the $7.50 needs" in my life where God first began to develop my faith and show me that He would be my Provider.

My next faith challenge was a bit larger. It came when I was down to choosing a college and sensing that I was to prepare for ministry. One more time I was asking God for absolute confirmation that this was His idea and not mine. I couldn't imagine daring to speak God's Word had I not known that God himself had called me to do it.

Now, needing $50 to send in my application, I prayed, "Lord, you and I both know that I do not have that $50. You know that I make enough money each week to keep gas in my car. You also know that I have always honored you with at least a tithe of my income, and I have not stopped giving to you to save up for these kinds of needs. This is such a momentous decision for me. So God, I am asking you one more time, if you are calling me to prepare for ministry, make that absolutely clear to me by unmistakably providing that $50 or providing me a way to earn it quickly." I told no one.

I will never forget the night, soon after I prayed that prayer, when I left the locker room at 9 o'clock after a late track meet. Walking towards my car in the dark, I could faintly make out the shadow of a man standing next to it. As I approached, he stuck out his hand and introduced himself as a representative from Fort Wayne Bible College.

He asked if I had sent in my registration yet. I answered, without telling him the specifics, "No, I'm still praying about it." And then he said, "Well, I just wanted you to know that the $50 for your registration is already in our office. All you need to do is send in your registration."

The impact of that answer to prayer was profound. More importantly, I went to college in the fall with a firm confidence that Fort Wayne Bible College was exactly where I was supposed to be.

Several years later, I felt led by God to pursue my Master's degree. Susan and I arrived at seminary in August 1982 with a $700 love offering in our pocket. School was going to cost me at least $5,000 in tuition and books per year. I didn't know how God was going to do it, but I had prayed very specifically that God would provide a way for us to handle those three years of seminary debt free, without my having to work full time so that I could give myself fully to my studies.

Susan got a job that essentially bought the groceries and covered the car payment, the rent and all the other bills. (We always say she earned her PHT . . . Put Hubby Through.) We finally landed on the idea of "sub-parenting" to pay my seminary bills. This meant that when parents on the north shore of Chicago went on vacation, they would usually call the seminary and ask for a couple to stay with their children. We'd live in their house, eat their food, drive their cars, spend their money, and on top of that, they'd pay us about $50 a day when they returned home. Such a deal! So each semester we would trust God to line us up enough jobs that we could pay off my seminary tuition semester-by-semester. And this He did faithfully.

Now mind you, there was always a bit of risk involved. Sometimes you would say "no" to one sub-parenting job in order to say "yes" to a better one. But let's say that "better one" cancelled on you at the last minute and of course, at that point, you not only were out of the job you had planned on, but you were also out of the one you had said "no" to, because someone else would have already filled it. It would have been a great way to run into trouble with your school bill. But never once in our first two years of seminary did anyone ever cancel a job we were depending on. So we breezed through my first and second year debt free, all the while honoring God by giving 15% of our income to the local church we attended.

NEVER ONCE IN OUR FIRST TWO YEARS OF SEMINARY DID ANYONE EVER CANCEL A JOB WE WERE DEPENDING ON

It was during my second year that a chapel speaker challenged the student body to make ourselves available for a possible career in overseas missions. He asked, as a first step of openness, if we would consider a short-term summer missions' assignment overseas. Then he asked for those who were willing to go, to stand and come forward. I stood and went forward that day with a whole host of other students. And I prayed, "God, I don't think I'm too serious about doing this. But if you want us to go overseas this summer, you're going to have to make it real clear. In fact, Lord, I'll know this is your will for us if you put the idea in Susan's heart. I'm not going to suggest it to her."

Of course, I knew I was safe because there was no way in the world Susan would want to leave the security of her job and our home to go overseas. Besides, it would require my having to raise about $3,000, while at the same time giving up a summer of making money for the next year's tuition and fees. Complicating matters even worse, were we to go overseas, Susan would have no income and she might even have to give up her job altogether if she asked for a two-month leave of absence. There were just way too many challenges to make this even a remote possibility for us. Yet I stood there acting as if I was serious about it and putting God up to a challenge I knew would be impossible. I just didn't know that He was getting ready to give us a lesson in Faith-Building 101. From my own experience I have learned this lesson: Be very careful what you pray for because God might just take you at your word and then you're stuck!

> LORD, I'LL KNOW THIS IS YOUR WILL FOR US IF YOU PUT THE IDEA IN SUSAN'S HEART

That evening Susan and I were headed from Chicago to Ft. Wayne for the weekend to visit my brother-in-law and sister. Making small talk in the car, Susan asked me, "How was your day?"

"Good!"

"What was chapel about today?"

"Oh, it was really good. This was our Missions Emphasis Week and the speaker today was great."

"What'd he speak about?"

"Oh, he talked about short-term summer missions and asked people to consider it."

It was then that my security loving, non-risk-taking wife almost caused us to have a major accident on the Eden's Expressway in Chicago when she said in her next breath: "You know, I've been thinking that you and I ought to consider going overseas this summer."

Needless to say, I was jaw-droppingly stunned! I proceeded to share with her the half-hearted commitment I had made just that morning, never thinking that I would see the time when it was "put up or shut up." But so soon that time had come and now I was stuck. I wanted to say, "God, I didn't mean it."

Though all the obstacles and impossibilities loomed in front of us, we made good on my promise to God and began to make plans for a summer mission's venture. From October of 1983 to June of 1984, we encountered some of the most severe challenges to our faith that we had ever known.

In April of 1984, after paying for our passports, we cried ourselves to sleep one night with only 89 cents in our checkbook and another week until payday. And I remember praying, "Lord, tonight I feel like this decision to go overseas is the dumbest choice I have ever made in my life. But we only made it because we felt that you wanted us to. So God, if this is your will, then you're going to have to work out every detail. If we've missed your leading, we'll gladly stay home."

All at once, amazing things began to happen. Susan went in to tell her boss what we were planning to do, fully prepared to lose her job, but he responded, "That sounds great. Good for you. I'd like you to train someone to take your place for those eight weeks. But when you come home, you've done such a good job that I'm going to give you a raise." Let me ask you: How often have you gotten a raise for requesting eight weeks off?

By the time we were to depart in June, more than enough money had come in to cover our expenses. The bank agreed to delay two months of car payments until we returned, without adding additional interest. Everything fell into place, with the exception of one major detail. With only a week left until departure, we were still looking for someone to sublet our apartment for eight weeks. We were praying, "Lord, please send us someone who needs a summer home."

Three days before we were to leave, we received a call from a person who was coming to summer school and was looking for an apartment to rent for a few weeks. When we inquired as to how long he would need it, the next miracle happened. He mentioned as the move-in date the exact day we were to leave. As for his departure date, I'll bet you can guess: the day before we were scheduled to arrive home! I'm not embellishing the story. It was unbelievable!

> BE VERY CAREFUL WHAT YOU PRAY FOR BECAUSE GOD MIGHT JUST TAKE YOU AT YOUR WORD AND THEN YOU'RE STUCK!

Only God could have orchestrated all these details. And guess what was happening to our faith? All those challenges were providing an opportunity for our faith to grow as we watched God come through time after time.

We had a great summer of ministry in Caracas, Venezuela. But, it was not lost on us that, if we were going to be able to pay for my fall semester of school, God was going to have to provide a full load of sub-parenting jobs. However, God had more surprises waiting for us. The first thing I discovered upon arriving back on campus in the fall was that the president of the seminary had raised enough money during the summer to pay the first semester's tuition for every student who had gone on a summer missions' project.

So, we started lining up sub-parenting jobs that fall to pay for the winter semester. And amazingly, in the one year that I was prepared to struggle the most financially due to the fact that we had had no summer employment, my entire school bill was paid off much sooner than in other years. In fact, by the end of April 1985, we had even been able to put away a couple hundred dollars for a vacation to Tucson that we were planning on taking upon my graduation in June. And we still had three sub-parenting jobs lined up!

I remember saying to Susan one evening, "This is unbelievable. We're not only going to come out of seminary debt free and enjoy a vacation to Tucson, but we'll probably have $1,000 to $1,500 in our pockets when we leave."

Remember how I told you that we never had a sub-parenting job cancel on us in three years? Once my tuition was paid and our vacation was covered, in rapid-fire succession the final three sub-parenting jobs called and said they were going to have to cancel. In fact, we never did another sub-parenting job. And God very clearly impressed upon my heart at the time that although He had promised to be my Provider, He had no plans to ever let me live beyond a level of needing to walk by faith in Him.

ALL THOSE CHALLENGES WERE PROVIDING AN OPPORTUNITY FOR OUR FAITH TO GROW

Without a doubt, more important and far more precious to me today than anything I ever learned through all my seminary courses, are the experiential lessons in faith development that God took me through. And I share some of my personal journey with you to say that His objective for each of us who have decided to follow Him is to develop our faith. And to do that, He has to present us with challenges that will stretch our faith. You might as well get used to the fact that you will come up against faith challenges. And when those challenges come, you have a choice: faith or fear, belief or doubt, obedience or disobedience.

Perhaps no passage in the Bible portrays that challenge and that choice better than Numbers 13:26 - 14:10. In this passage, Moses sent 12 spies to check out the land that God had promised to give to the Israelites. The problem was that as these 12 guys were out surveying the land, they recognized some giant-sized obstacles in front of them. At this point they were confronted with a question: "Do I believe God is bigger than these giants we're facing? What's it going to be - faith or fear?" You may be facing that question in your life today.

In this story, 10 of the spies responded in fear. Only two, Joshua and Caleb, had the faith to believe that God would give them what He had promised and were willing to do whatever it took. It's an incredible story that lays out some major principles we need to understand when facing the faith or fear dilemma.

When I first taught these principles to the people I pastor, we were in the midst of a $7 million stewardship campaign. That was a giant staring us down. But as we magnified the Lord and His promises, our people sacrificed, the miracle happened for us as a church, and people were blessed in their lives financially as they stepped out to new levels of faith in their financial giving. The same will happen for you, your family, and your church if you're willing to walk by faith instead of fear in light of the challenge that faces you.

Principle #1:
God plays no Favorites, only Faithorites!

This has always been His way and always will be. God doesn't respond to our prayers based upon our importance, our position, or our status. The only thing He recognizes is faith and obedience. When I am walking in faith and obedience to Him, I am walking in an environment that makes me a candidate for His blessing. When I am not walking in faith and obedience, I am no longer in that environment of blessing. He plays no favorites, only faithorites.

2 Chronicles 16:9 says, "For the eyes of the Lord range throughout the earth to strengthen those whose hearts are fully

committed to Him." You see, He doesn't look at names. He looks at hearts. God is always looking for hearts of faith and commitment.

What's interesting about this story is that all 12 of the spies had the same opportunity to experience God's blessing. It wasn't as if God just liked Joshua and Caleb more than the others. Had the other 10 responded in faith, they would have known the same blessings that Joshua and Caleb later enjoyed. But they chose fear instead of faith and that is what made all the difference. God plays no favorites, only faithorites. Are you one of His faithorites?

Principle #2:
Our choice can only be proven
against the backdrop of a challenge!

That's a consistent theme throughout the entire Bible. In 1 Peter 1:6-7, the apostle Peter is writing to some fellow believers who are going through trials and challenges to their faith. He says to them, "These have come so that your faith - of greater worth than gold . . . may be proved genuine . . . "

HE HAS TO

PRESENT US WITH

CHALLENGES THAT

WILL STRETCH

OUR FAITH

I think these 10 spies went to check out that land assuming that if God meant to give it to them, it wasn't going to require any sweat on their part. But then they were presented with a challenge in the form of some giants and they began to lose sight of what God had promised He would do. God was saying, "I was just checking to see whether there's any faith in the camp."

The only way He can give us a faith check-up is to present us with a challenge so that He can see what our response will be. With respect to our finances, I believe God uses the principle of tithing to test our faith. Some people tithe in spite of dire circumstances because they have faith that God will provide. They know it's their job to obey. Others assume that if God wanted them to tithe, He would remove all of their financial hassles so they could or so that it would be easier. They think that because they have a challenge, God doesn't expect them to give. But the truth is the exact opposite. It's the challenge that demonstrates whether our choice is faith or fear, belief or doubt.

Principle #3:
Our perspective is always more important than our problem!

> HE DOESN'T LOOK AT NAMES. HE LOOKS AT HEARTS. GOD IS ALWAYS LOOKING FOR HEARTS OF FAITH AND COMMITMENT.

The 10 spies who missed out on the Promised Land did not forfeit their rightful inheritance because of their problem. They missed out because of their *perspective* on the problem. They had a "we can't" perspective. They said in Numbers 13:31, "We can't attack those people; they are stronger than we are." And because they had a faithless perspective, they allowed a problem that should not have defeated them to prevent them from attaining what they otherwise could have attained . . . all because of their perspective.

Little Bobby knew how important perspective was. One day his father came into the front room and saw Bobby gazing at the street through the big end of the telescope. Correcting him, the dad said, "Son, that's not the way you look through a telescope. If you use it that way, you make the objects look smaller. A telescope is to make things look bigger."

But Bobby smiled and said, "Daddy, the bully who's always beating me up is out on the street. I turned the telescope around because he's my main problem, and I want to see him smaller than he really is." Smart kid!

When you're presented with a faith challenge, it matters a whole lot which end of the telescope you turn on the problem and which end you turn on God. What we want to do is magnify God and minimize the problem. That's why Psalm 34:3 says, "Magnify the Lord!" It's a word that means to "make large." But many of us magnify the problem and in turn minimize God. Particularly is that true when it comes to financial problems.

Yet, what do we find when we turn the telescope of God's promise on our financial problems? Philippians 4:19 says, "And my God will meet all of your needs according to His glorious riches in Christ Jesus." When understood in context, Paul was magnifying the vastness of God's resources to encourage us to give, even if we have needs. Because it's through our giving, even though we're faced with financial challenges, that we prove our faith in God's ability to provide.

IT'S THE CHALLENGE THAT DEMONSTRATES WHETHER OUR CHOICE IS FAITH OR FEAR.

Principle #4:
What you see is what you get!

One person's problems are often another person's possibilities. One person's obstacles are another person's opportunities. What you see determines your response to what you see and this in turn determines what you get. It's all a matter of whether you see through eyes of faith or fear!

So 10 of these guys said, "We can't go in there and take the land. Those giants are bigger than what we are!" In verse 33 they said, "We seemed like grasshoppers in our own eyes and we looked the same to them." And thus they got what their view produced.

But two members of the group saw the obstacles in light of the size of their God and said, "It doesn't matter how big we are or how big they are. The question is: *How big of a God do we serve?*"

LIVING AT A HIGHER LEVEL OF FAITH

And they received what their giant-sized view of God could produce.

You see, when we allow the problems to overshadow the possibilities, we end up seeing through the eyes of fear. And when we see through eyes of fear, we underestimate what God can do. It's so important that you understand this principle: *God will allow people to limit Him.* And by limiting Him, I do not mean to imply that you and I can in any way subtract anything from His essential nature. But we can limit His activity among us depending upon whether we respond in faith or fear. Mark 6:5,6 sounds this ominous note from Jesus' ministry in His hometown one day, "He could not do any miracles there . . . and he was amazed at their lack of faith."

Principle #5:
God will allow our choice to stand!

MANY OF US MAGNIFY THE PROBLEM AND IN TURN MINIMIZE GOD

It's amazing that God treated each one in the Israelite community according to their choice. Those who responded in fear and disbelief reaped the consequences of their choice. Those few who responded in faith got to experience the Promised Land.

But here's the point: When they found out later that because of their lack of faith they were not going to get to experience the Promised Land that they otherwise would have known had they responded in faith, they all started weeping and wailing and saying, "Okay God, we didn't mean it. Please let us have another chance. We didn't know that our lack of faith would make us miserable." Numbers 14 is a sad chapter because God allowed their choice to stand.

We've probably all been there before. One of our children perhaps asked to have a friend stay over Friday night, but meanwhile they were involved in some behavior that made us question whether they should receive that privilege. So we issued the challenge: "You can choose to keep up these antics or you can choose to respect what I have said. But I just want you to know that if you keep misbehaving, you're also choosing not to have a friend over Friday night."

Of course, they then went ahead and behaved badly one more time just to see if we meant it, only to find out, too late, that we did. When they received the promised punishment, the pleading began. "I didn't mean it. Give me another chance. Please, if you give me one more chance I promise I'll do better." But sadly, the one more chance has already come and gone.

That's why it's so important for you to understand that when the moment of faith presents itself and you don't take it, you forever lose what could have been yours. To be sure, there will be other challenges, but you can never have back the one you didn't take.

So where is God challenging you in your faith right now? Where are you afraid to step out because you're not sure He'll provide? Where might you be holding back in giving to His cause because you can't figure out how He'll provide?

WHEN WE ALLOW THE PROBLEMS TO OVERSHADOW THE POSSIBILITIES, WE END UP SEEING THROUGH THE EYES OF FEAR

I promise you, as you decide to live at a higher level of faith, you are going to be challenged and stretched at times in your financial world. God is going to ask you to give up some things you don't think you can live without. He is going to put you in situations where you have no way out but what He provides. And at that point it will be a choice between faith and fear. But let me encourage you: Once you have passed the financial test and seen God provide, your faith will go to a whole new level.

Father, I never want to be afraid to step out in faith no matter what you ask me to do. I don't want to miss out on the opportunities to see you work in powerful ways in my life. Right now, I claim you as my Provider, no matter what my need may be. I submit my financial resources to you. I covenant to return the tithe to you, no matter how difficult my financial situation may be. I believe with all my heart that you will provide all my needs according to your glorious riches in Christ Jesus. In Jesus name, Amen.

As important as it is that we pass the test of faith in our finances, it's even more important that we pass the test of faith in our families. The greatest gift we can give our children is a legacy of faith. That's the topic of the next chapter.

CHAPTER NINE

*"Love the Lord your God with all your heart and with all
your soul and with all your strength. These commandments
that I give you today are to be upon your hearts.
Impress them upon your children."*
DEUTERONOMY 6: 5-7

LEAVING A LEGACY OF FAITH

Each week, I eagerly look forward to the arrival of my *Sports
Illustrated* (except for the annual Swimsuit Issue, which my wife
promptly shreds). Usually, I immediately read the article on the
back page, written by Rick Reilly and appropriately entitled, "The
Life of Reilly." Not long ago, Reilly's article focused on John
Elway, the former Denver Bronco quarterback who retired in 1999
as the winningest quarterback in NFL history.

The article began, "After he retired, he took all that cool, all
that glory and all that cash, and galloped into the sunset. But
somebody ran off with John Elway's happily ever after. Since he
quit playing, lucky number 7 has hit the worst losing streak of his
life: His father died, most of his business ventures flopped,
recently his twin sister, Jana, died and then things on the home
front began to cave in."

Elway, now 42, says, "When you're a quarterback, you're in
control. The football's in your hand, and it's fourth-and-12, and
if the wideout doesn't take the right route, I'm going to run
around and make things happen. But now, things go wrong and I
don't have the football anymore."

This past June, Elway's wife of 18 years, Janet, moved out and
took their four kids with her. She says, "It's like we were lonely

inside our marriage. It was time for drastic measures." Reilly quips, tongue in cheek, "All of a sudden it looked as if Elway could hold his Hall of Fame induction ceremony in a phone booth."

But with the loss of his father and his sister and the realization that he was losing his family, Elway began his most important comeback to date. He began to invest on the home front like never before. He began to go to Janet's rented house and pull weeds in her garden when she wasn't home. He even went to the mall with her. She says, "John hadn't been in a mall for 16 years!" He sent her roses every week, opened her car doors, and started hanging out with the kids.

WHAT ARE THE

MOST IMPORTANT

INVESTMENTS YOU

CAN MAKE IN YOUR

CHILDREN'S LIVES?

Elway says, "Them leaving kind of woke me up. It was like a two-by-four to the heart. I want to put my family first from now on."

As the article concludes, Elway says, "I was driving by Six Flags the other day, and it hit me: *I've never taken my family to the amusement park!* So we're going, even if I have to rent it for a day. Or even if I have to tell people, 'Sorry, I can't sign autographs today. I'm with my family.'" And then he says, "I remembered something - I happen to *love* roller coasters."[1]

As I read that article, I found my heart saying, "Way to go, John!" There's just something that fires me up, particularly when a man turns his heart towards home and begins to realize that the investment of his time and energy into his wife and children is the greatest investment he can ever make. The returns on that investment are huge for years to come.

Think about it for a moment if you're a parent. What are the most important investments you can make in your children's lives?

It's great when we focus our time and energy on our children, have a great relationship with them, go to the amusement parks, etc. But what are the most important investments we can make? What is the end we have in mind for our children? Fifty years from now, when I'm gone and my investment is returning dividends in the lives of my children and their children and grandchildren, what do I hope the return on my investment looks like?

I did some daydreaming about this some time ago. I thought: *If fifty years from now I'm gone and I could check in on my kids, incognito, what would I hope to see?* Playing this out a little bit, I thought, "Wow, there's my daughter Kathryn, now 66, and her four grown children and 10 grandchildren. She's still a master at interior design (even though she didn't build that 17 bathroom mansion she dreamed of living in). And look, she still enjoys cutting the grandkids' hair.

WHAT WOULD MAKE ME MOST EXCITED 50 YEARS FROM NOW WHEN IT COMES TO MY CHILDREN?

"There's Jonathon, 64, now on the other side of his NBA aspirations, and his three grown children and their nine grandchildren. He loves to take the grandkids fishing in his boat (even though it's not the yacht in Florida that he had dreamed about when he was young).

"And Victoria, she just turned 60. She's got eight kids and is working on about 15 grandchildren (she's got that mom thing down).

"Look at Nathan. He's 57, has two children, and several grandkids whom he wows with his 51 snakes (he says that's what he's going to have, and even though I've warned him that he might have a hard time finding a wife if he insists on having 51 snakes, he's assured me that he'll just keep them in a separate room and keep the door closed)."

But I thought, playing this out further, what would make me most excited 50 years from now when it comes to my children? Oh, sure I would be so glad if all of my children were happy and healthy and had good marriages and strong homes. I would hope that they were successful in their chosen professions and were deeply satisfied with their lives. I want all of that for them!

But more than anything else, far above anything else, I would want to check in and see that my kids were leading godly lives, sold out to Jesus Christ, strong in their faith, strong in character and compassionate towards the needs of others and doing all that they could to make a difference for Christ. That would be the greatest return!

Beyond that, I would want to know that their children and grandchildren were equally devoted to Christ . . . in other words, a legacy of faith by which I knew that future generations of my offspring were living their lives for eternity. I can't think of any greater return I'd want on my investment on the home front than that.

Parents, how many of you would rather your kids just be successful in this life and miss out on eternity? Maybe some of you aren't sure about eternity and aren't convinced that faith in Jesus Christ is the only way to secure that eternity. But just for a minute, assume that that is true. Can you think of anything so important on this earth for which you'd want your child to sacrifice an eternity in heaven? Wouldn't you rather know, no matter what happens in this life, that your children and grandchildren and great-grandchildren were going to be in heaven because they lived their lives with a strong faith in Jesus Christ? I can't think of anything I could want for my kids more important than that.

So, the question is, what's the surest way to know that 50 years from now, that scenario will be alive and well in my family? What is the surest way to know that my investment on the home front is going to result in spiritually sensitive children who are devoted to Jesus Christ?

Bruce Wilkinson writes in his book, *First Hand Faith*, about being at a conference one day when a friend, pointing to a young man on the other side of the auditorium, asked him, "Do you know who that is? That's Rob so-and-so." He was the son of a famous Christian leader and internationally known speaker, whom Bruce had respected all his life. Bruce writes, "The first thought that came to my mind was, 'I want to talk to him. I'd really like to find out what it was like to grow up in such an incredible home with a father like that.'"

So during the next break, Bruce made his way over to the young man and introduced himself. He said, "I'm Bruce Wilkinson and I've been an admirer of your father for years. I'd love to know what it was like growing up in your dad's home."

Bruce says, "That young man's mouth fell open. He stared at me with cold eyes for a moment, as if trying to get his emotions under control. Finally, he squeezed out, 'I hate my father. I hate God.' Then he swore a blue streak, muttered, 'Stay away from me,' and stalked out of the room."

Bruce adds, "You could have picked my jaw up from off the floor. I was stunned that the son of one of the most famous Christian leaders had just cursed God and said that he hated his father! How on earth could that happen? How did he get to that point? As I pondered it, my thoughts turned to my own family." He concludes, "I couldn't think of anything worse than somebody walking up to one of my kids some day, asking if they were the son or daughter of Bruce Wilkinson, and being sworn at for mentioning my name. And my children rejecting the Lord I love and serve? How could I keep that from happening?"[2]

It was in his search for that answer that Bruce Wilkinson discovered a concept in the Bible that is really the seed thought for this chapter. As he began to study the Bible, he noticed a particular phenomenon happening time and time again. In one generation you might have had a man or woman who was totally devoted to the Lord and, what I call, walking in a first-hand faith, personally acquainted with the Lord and seeing Him work in mighty ways in his/her life.

When that person died, the next generation wasn't quite as devoted. It's like they had a second-hand faith. They still believed in God, but rather than experiencing Him personally, they lived more off the fact that mom or dad had had that experience with the Lord. For them it was more of a religious thing than it was a real heart-felt relationship with the Lord. And then, by the time the third generation arose, it's as if they were totally removed from any devotion to the Lord at all and had become completely secularized in their living and thinking.

WHEN THAT PERSON DIED, THE NEXT GENERATION WASN'T QUITE AS DEVOTED. IT'S LIKE THEY HAD A SECOND-HAND FAITH.

We see this occurring in Joshua's day. Joshua was a great spiritual leader in ancient Israel and in Joshua 24:31, the Bible says, "Israel served the Lord throughout the lifetime of Joshua and of the elders who outlived him and who had experienced everything the Lord had done for Israel." (Do you see the first-hand experience of their faith)? But also involved in that community of faith were another group of people who hadn't been around to experience what Joshua and the elders had experienced first-hand. They still believed in God but it was more of a faith based upon what mom and dad had seen God do, not a faith based on first-hand experience.

So once Joshua and the elders passed on, this then left a second generation of people who had only a second-hand knowledge of what God had done. They hadn't been there to see it personally; their parents had only told them about it. But here's the point: *while a second-hand faith may believe all the right things about God, it has no first-hand experience with God* and transfer of that second-hand faith to the third generation then becomes problematic.

Judges 2:10, which captures the third generation after Joshua and the elders are gone, says this, "After that whole generation had been gathered to their fathers, another generation grew up, who knew neither the Lord nor what he had done for Israel." These folks not only didn't know the Lord, they didn't even remember the stories that their parents had told them about Him.

Wilkinson's question was, "How do we keep that from happening in our own families? How can we live with a fair degree of certainty that the investment we make in our children is going to return generations of children who grow up with first-hand faith?" In answer to that question, Wilkinson came up with a concept called the three chairs, which I have adopted and modified for my use here.

WHILE A SECOND-HAND FAITH MAY BELIEVE ALL THE RIGHT THINGS ABOUT GOD, IT HAS NO FIRST-HAND EXPERIENCE WITH GOD

Understanding the Three Chairs

Chair #1: I call this "The Chair of First-hand Experience." This represents the person who has a personal first-hand faith in Jesus Christ, a faith that shapes everything about him/her. This person prays for God's guidance on a regular basis, experiences God's leading and answers to prayer, makes decisions based upon the wisdom and insight of the Word of God, takes his directives from the Word of God for all of life, and though not perfect, obviously, demonstrates consistent character and growing obedience to the Lord. This person doesn't compartmentalize his faith; it shapes everything about him, whether at work, home, school, etc.

The first chair person often carries on a running dialogue in his mind and heart with the Lord from the moment he gets up in the morning until the time he goes to bed. That relationship is the most significant and precious thing about his life. And because it is, that person has a vital relationship with the Church of Jesus Christ and believes that the Church really is the hope of the world. The first chair person lives to influence others with the love of Christ.

Now, to whatever degree that first chair may or may not be representative of my life, it has just never occurred to me to shoot for anything less than to live in the first chair. There's no spiritual life, joy, or action in any of the other chairs. I want to experience the Lord first-hand.

IT HAS JUST NEVER OCCURRED TO ME TO SHOOT FOR ANYTHING LESS THAN TO LIVE IN THE FIRST CHAIR. THERE'S NO SPIRITIUAL LIFE, JOY, OR ACTION IN ANY OF THE OTHER CHAIRS.

Over the years, God has given me many first-hand encounters of His power and leadings in my life. In fact, the only reason I am a preacher of the gospel today is because of a very clear and compelling call from God to lay down my other aspirations and give my life in service to Him. I've often thought that I could find real joy in teaching and coaching except for the fact that God has called me to preach and has never removed that call from my life, even when I've wondered if He made a mistake.

God has graciously granted to me many specific answers to prayer. Often He has provided for specific needs I have brought to Him in prayer. He has given specific directions to questions I have asked. I have known His comfort in times of sorrow. I have experienced His strength when I had no more strength left. I have known His cleansing grace and tender mercy as He has gently nudged me to further growth. The fact is, I couldn't choose to forget Him or what He's done for me if I wanted to because I have experienced Him first-hand. And were you to put a gun to my head today and tell me to deny that these things have happened, I would tell you, "Pull the trigger! I will never deny Him."

While I would never suggest that I am a paragon of first-chair faith, nonetheless I can tell you that I have tasted something of first-hand experience with God and it has only made me hungry for more. And I can think of nothing that I want more for my wife and my children and the generations of their children to follow than that they sit in the first chair, the chair of first-hand experience with God.

I HAVE TESTED SOMETHING OF FIRST-HAND EXPERIENCE WITH GOD AND IT HAS ONLY MADE ME HUNGRY FOR MORE.

Chair #2: This is "The Chair of Casual Acquaintance." It represents a person who has put his faith in Jesus. He believes that Jesus is who He said He is and has trusted Him for the forgiveness of his sins. But that's about as far as it goes.

Second chair people are known as Sunday-only Christians. They made a decision for Christ somewhere in the past, so they content themselves with the fact that it's taken care of. The problem is that this decision has very little to do with the rest of their life, Monday thru Saturday. In making personal and business decisions, they don't really operate from the principles of God's Word. They don't really concern themselves with demonstrating godly character, speech and behavior in all they do. If they were put on trial for being a Christian, it's doubtful they'd be found guilty because there wouldn't be enough evidence to convict them.

They run their business like everyone else. Their character is inconsistent at best. Their first inclination in handling problems is to figure it out on their own rather than to seek God about it. They rarely study His Word to see what He has to say. Their values are more world-shaped then Word-shaped. Their commitment to the Church is minimal at best. They have very little first-hand experience of the Lord's guidance, power and answers to prayer in their own lives. They marvel that some people seem to experience God more on a first-hand basis, but they assume it's because they are just more religious people. While they might claim to know God, they give very little evidence of, in fact, knowing Him!

Not long ago, a close friend of mine shared some frustration he was having with a competitor in town. Many of this man's employees were leaving him and coming to my friend with the same story. They would say, "This guy is just flat out crooked in his business dealings and defends himself by telling us that we don't know how to run a business."

The sad news is that this man has, for years, given public lip service to the Gospel. If you were to ask him if he is a Christian, he would say, "Sure. I accepted Christ into my life when I was a kid." But you wouldn't have any evidence of that fact based upon how he runs his life and business. And sadder still is the fact that many non-Christians with whom he has dealings can't believe how crooked he is either.

Now to be fair, not every second-chair Christian is necessarily a poor role model, bent on living a crooked life. Many in the second-chair are great people. It's just that their faith is something of a back burner issue, rather than the front burner priority in their lives. And because it's back burner, it doesn't seem to heat up anyone around them. So if our children live around this kind of Sunday-only faith all the time, guess what? It's not going to produce first-chair kids. In fact, it probably won't even produce another Sunday-only Christian. It usually leads to a third chair type of person.

Chair #3: I call this "The Chair of Spiritual Disinterest." This represents those whom, as I said, have become pretty secularized in their thinking. They simply have no experience with or expectation of a God who does mighty works, who answers prayer, who can lead you personally, whose Word is alive and active, and who loves you intimately. Consequently, He is a non-entity in this person's life.

This chair may even represent someone reading this book. Perhaps you find your previous disinterest in God turning to interest. And if so, that's great! That itself is evidence of God awakening you to the first vestiges of faith in your life. Take my word for it, there's nothing more exciting in the entire world than experiencing the living God, who wants to know you personally and who wants to reveal Himself to you through a first-hand faith.

But now, having briefly defined those three chairs, ask yourself as a parent: "Which of those chairs do I want my kids to sit in?" Now, don't miss this point: *The surest way for any of us to raise first-chair children is to make sure we're first-chair parents!* That is the greatest investment we can make on the home front. Jesus asked a poignant question in Matthew 16:26, "What good will it be for a man if he gains the whole world, yet forfeits his soul?"

YOU WILL NOT PRODUCE SPIRITUAL HEAT IN YOUR CHILDREN IF THERE'S NO BURNING PASSION AND HUNGER FOR SPIRITUAL GROWTH IN YOUR OWN LIFE

Think about it. What good will it be for your son or daughter if you teach them how to gain the whole world (and we certainly want them to succeed) and yet they live and die in the third chair, primarily because they never saw in you a person who was serious about first-chair living? You maybe invested everywhere else in your child's life except there. I want to encourage you to make your greatest investment that of passing along a first-chair faith! So how do we do that? Let's look at several keys to producing first-chair children.

Producing First-Chair Children

Key #1:
Be passionate about and absolutely committed to your own spiritual growth!

This means you have to move your own spiritual growth and faith development on to the front burner of your life. You will not produce spiritual heat in your children if there's no burning passion and hunger for spiritual growth in your own life. Begin to study the Word of God. Start to pray about the concerns in your life and in the lives of your children and let them know some of the things you're talking to God about. Let them hear you and see you praying about your concerns.

And this isn't about being super-spiritual. I'm pretty sure my daughter, Kathryn, wouldn't be too excited to see her dad down on his knees praying for her at a volleyball game. No, it's about being spiritually authentic and letting the things of God be a normal part of your life and conversation.

Personally, I'm trying to be more cognizant of turning to God whenever a need presents itself. This past Labor Day, we met Susan's folks out in Mt. Pleasant, IA, at the Old Threshers Reunion. We spent the day walking around and when it was time to leave, knowing that my father-in-law was going to Mayo Clinic for testing in a few days, I just thought, "Let's pray for him." So there, tucked away on a street corner by our van, Susan and I, along with Grandma and my two youngest kids, huddled around Grandpa and asked God to bless him, to heal him, and to help us discover what was wrong.

When I finished praying for him, he had tears in his eyes and I had tears in mine because there were my children, about up to his waist, with their arms wrapped around him as we prayed for Grandpa. It was a beautiful picture. But beyond that, it was a moment that communicated to our children that it's okay to bring our needs to God at any time and at any place.

Be passionate about pursuing your own spiritual growth and developing your faith. Study the Bible. Set aside time to pray. Read good Christian literature that can help you grow. Listen to teaching tapes. There are a myriad of ways you can invest in your own growth. As you crank up the spiritual heat in your own life, the more likely you will be to warm up your children.

YOU DEVELOP AND DISPLAY A FIERCE LOVE FOR GOD AND IT WILL RUB OFF. THAT'S HOW THE TRANSFER OF LOYALTY WORKS.

Key #2:
Model the values you hope to instill!

It's one of the cardinal rules of passing along your faith. More is always caught than taught so model what you hope to instill because the truth is you will instill what you model! Robert Fulghum said, "Don't worry that your children never listen to you; worry that they are always watching you." It's my all-time number one passage that I have turned to again and again when it comes to raising my children. Deuteronomy 6:5-7 says, "Love the Lord your God with all your heart and with all your soul and with all your strength. These commandments that I give you today are to be upon your hearts. Impress them upon your children." Mark it down. *You can only impress upon your children that which has first made an impression on you!*

Notice where leaving a lasting impression begins. You love the Lord your God with everything you have and let His Word and His thoughts and ways be upon your heart. You develop and display a fierce love for God and it will rub off. That's how the transfer of loyalty works.

LIVING IN THE FIRST

CHAIR IS NOT SOME

SORT OF PROGRAM.

IT'S A LIFESTYLE!

In other words, I didn't have to teach my kids to like the Green Bay Packers. One of these days it may dawn on them that being a Packer fan in football is as self-defeating as being a Cub fan in baseball. But some day when people ask them, "How did you ever get started rooting for the Packers?" their answer will be, "Because my dad liked them and he forced us against our wills to like them." No, they'll more likely say, "Because we lived in Illinois and thought the Bears were our only other option." The point is, they've just sort of picked up what they've been around. Model the values you hope to instill because you are instilling what you model.

Your walk talks all the time! So the cashier gives you an extra dollar of change. Do you tell her and make it right? For first chair people, it's no question. First chair people know your walk talks and your talk talks but your walk talks a whole lot louder than your talk talks! So, are the values upon which you've based your life derived from the Word of God or do you just have a sliding scale of convenience that guides how you're going to live?

Key #3:
Bring all of life into your faith!

You're not trying to bring your faith into your life. Rather, you're trying to bring your life into your faith. This is why the Bible says, "These commandments that I give you today are to be upon your hearts. Impress them on your children." How? Verse 7 goes on, "Talk about them when you sit at home and when you walk along the road, when you lie down and when you get up."

Verses 8 and 9 say, in essence, "Keep reminders of God's Word in front of you all the time." In other words, living in the first chair is not some sort of program. It's a lifestyle! That's not to say that you shouldn't have set times when you might sit down with your family and talk about God's Word, pray together or read the Bible together. But God tells us here that all of life is the classroom. We must engage those teaching moments each day. When you're watching television together, when you're driving down the road, when you're just sitting on the bed talking to each other, etc.

> WE HAVE TO FIGHT PASSIVITY. WHENEVER WE FAIL TO STEP IN AND LEAD, SOMEONE OR SOMETHING ELSE IS GOING TO FILL THAT VOID.

There have been some wonderful moments in our family when we have prayed together and seen God answer prayer. What's happening in those times is that we are, in essence, making room in that first chair and saying, "Let's all sit here and see what God will do."

When we moved to a new home in a different school district a few years ago, the first few days of school were really tough for our oldest daughter, Kathryn. She was just starting seventh grade and had to make all new friends. Several days in a row she came home in tears because she hadn't made any friends.

One day, just before I went out the door for work, the Lord nudged my heart to pray with Kathryn about finding a friend that day. And so I asked Him specifically to give her a good day and to provide one friend for her. That day she came home excited because some new friendships had formed, and she never looked back after that. You see, that wasn't me telling her about my experience with God. That was Kathryn experiencing God's answer first-hand! That's what can happen when you bring all of life into your faith.

Key #4:
Proactively engage in your child's spiritual development!

In other words, fight off passivity when it comes to building and reinforcing spiritual values in your child's life. Dads, particularly, this is a huge issue for us. Many of us feel so confident and competent in leading our businesses and such, but when we come home we check out and don't give our families the kind of spiritual leadership they need.

We have to fight passivity. Whenever we fail to step in and lead, someone or something else is going to fill that void. So are you going to leave the development of your child's spiritual values to the television, the Internet, the locker room, boyfriends and girlfriends? Where else is that first-hand faith going to come from? Who else is going to make that investment? It's not enough for your wife to do it alone. When it comes to your teenagers, who else is going to reinforce God's standards when it comes to dating? Many dads don't have a clue about who their son or daughter is going out with or what's going on. Get involved. Know what is going on in your child's life. Keep the communication lines open and set boundaries. Let them know what's expected. Pray with and for them.

January 2002 ushered my wife and me into a whole new "teenage season." That's when our oldest daughter turned 16. We had told her she couldn't date until she was 16. But I had also made it clear that when she started "going out" on dates, that young man and I were going to have a chat. Well, soon enough, the time arrived.

I sat down with this young man who had come to take my daughter out and I think I was as nervous as he was! But I had my speech prepared. I, in essence, told him that my daughter was worth a billion dollars to me and I was wrestling with the whole idea of letting someone else run around with my billion dollars.

So, I said, "Here's what I expect: (1) Treat here like a lady; (2) Treat here like she's mine, not yours; (3) Drive your car like you're protecting my treasure; (4) Bring her home on time, and (5) Keep your hands off her body (no further explanation needed)." It must have worked because Kathryn later told me, "Dad, I can't even get him to hug me!" I was like, "Good boy!"

But that's what I'm talking about. Get involved. Continue to paint the picture of what it means to live with a first-chair faith, what it means to take God's Word seriously. Don't try to do it from the second or third chair. Get in that first chair yourself and from there, invite your kids to sit on that chair with you so that they experience what God can do first hand. It's the most important investment you can make on the home front. God help us all to raise first chair families!

Lord Jesus, the greatest desire of my heart is that I live a first-chair faith and instill that type of faith in my children. Wherever I have fallen short, forgive me! Wherever I need help to develop that kind of faith, help me! I want to give you more than just casual acquaintance or indifference. Lord, I want a living experience with you! That's the only thing that will satisfy my soul. Please speak to me, lead me and empower me to take fresh steps of faith with you, and in so doing, to impact those whom I love the most. In Jesus name, Amen!

There's nothing like living a life of faith and going to new levels of faith as you walk with Jesus. It's my prayer that this book has aided you in that quest, and whet your appetite for new steps of growth. And be assured that as you take those steps, you will find yourself enjoying the payoffs of higher level living. You'll find more on that in the last chapter.

CHAPTER TEN

"Be strong and courageous.
Do not be terrified; do not be discouraged, for
the Lord our God will be with you wherever you go."
JOSHUA 1:9

ENJOYING FAITH'S PAYOFF

If there was one chore I hated when I was a kid, it was being forced to hoe my mom's garden. I never liked the kind of things that were planted there and had no intention of eating them anyway. And I'd let Mom know that: "If I don't plan on eating any of this stuff, why do I have to go out and hoe?" But that wasn't all. The ground was rock hard and half the time the weeds were so thick that I couldn't see where the rows were anyway.

I hated working in that garden and so I made life miserable for my mom whenever she asked me to toil out there. My brothers and I would say, "Well we're just going to swing away and if we knock out your plants with the weeds, we aren't going to care." We were sweet, lovable, adorable kids.

But why is it, I ask myself, that one of my favorite memories from that same period of time in my life is when my grandfather would hire me, along with my brothers and several of my cousins, to hoe weeds from his sugar beet field? Often times that was a three-day job of long hours, walking row after row of beets, hoeing weeds. And yet I was always ready for that. Same situation, same job, but two different reactions and two different levels of motivation. What was the difference? Well, the difference was that in one scenario there was no payoff of any consequence. I didn't see the fact that I got to eat what my mom's garden produced as a payoff. That was more like punishment. What kid likes all those vegetables?

But with my grandpa's field, that was a completely different story. You see, I can count on one hand the number of times our family got to eat out while I was growing up. But when we were hoeing grandpa's field, we knew that for three days running, at lunch time he was going to pile 8 to 10 of us cousins in the back of his pick-up and drive us to the A&W Root Beer stand. There I would gorge myself on a delicious cheeseburger, onion rings and a cold frosty mug of root beer. There was nothing better . . . and to get that reward three days in a row was like heaven. I concluded as a kid, "There will be A&W's in heaven!" (Incidentally, for those who have asked me, I have concluded that there will be no golf in heaven. The Bible says there will be no weeping, wailing and gnashing of teeth. So golf is clearly out!)

HE HAS PROMISED PAYOFFS TO THOSE WHO WILL TAKE THE JOURNEY AND WALK WITH HIM BY FAITH

But the point is, the A&W was a huge payoff that motivated us to chop those weeds. We could almost taste what was coming as we walked the long rows each day. And then, to top it all off, at the end of the three days when the job was done, Grandpa would gather us around and give us each a brand new $10 bill. Man that was the payday! That was worth everything. I felt like the richest kid in town. Put the payoff in front of me and I could have walked those fields all summer long. But take the payoff out of the picture and it was a tough sell!

The God who made us knows that we're wired up that way. That's why He has promised payoffs to those who will take the journey and walk with Him by faith. He knew that sometimes on our faith journey we would get tired, grow weary, experience setbacks and disappointments along the way and sometimes wonder if it was worth it. And were there no promise of payoffs along the way, He knew it would be easy for us to throw in the towel.

But, there are payoffs and God intends for those spiritual A&W trips and the knowledge of a payday up ahead to be tremendous motivators as we seek to live by faith and go to higher and higher levels in our walk with Him. So I want to conclude this book by looking at four payoffs that can keep you motivated as you seek to live by faith.

Payoff #1:
An expanded spiritual comfort zone!

This is akin to the athlete who has been working hard and begins to experience the payoff of a higher level of performance: more points, faster times, better scores, stronger muscles, more wins. That's motivating and it's that payoff that can make him work that much harder. So it is in the Christian life. John Ortberg writes, "Most of us have an area that might be called our 'spiritual comfort zone,' which is the area where we feel most comfortable trusting God. When God calls us to go beyond our spiritual comfort zone, we begin to feel nervous or uncomfortable. We would prefer not to go outside the zone until we feel better about it."[1]

ONCE WE FORCE OURSELVES OUTSIDE THAT ZONE, AND EXPERIENCE THE PAYOFF OF WHAT GOD DOES, OUR COMFORT ZONE EXPANDS AND THAT'S MOTIVATING

But, once we force ourselves outside that zone, and experience the payoff of what God does, our comfort zone expands and that's motivating. For instance, we might feel comfortable talking about God with church friends, but nervous about explaining our faith to someone who does not believe. We might be comfortable in our current job, but anxious about the possibility that God wants us to do some vocational realignment. We might have enough faith to pray about the hurt someone is causing us, but actually confronting the person would make us cringe.[2] We might feel good about the fact that we have at least started giving God a little of the leftovers from our income, but becoming an off-the-top tither is quite a stretch. We might feel comfortable sharing with a friend that we have become a Christian, but making a public profession through baptism seems so scary.

There is only one way to increase your spiritual comfort zone, and acquiring more information alone will not do it. You will have to, at some point, follow God's lead and take a step of faith. And that's never comfortable. You'll have to face a bit of discomfort, anxiety and fear. That's why God says in Joshua 1:9, "Be strong and courageous. Do not be terrified; do not be discouraged, for the Lord your God will be with you wherever you go." God will be with you each step of the way, and as you step out, your comfort zone will be expanded. You'll grow and you'll be more motivated in your faith as you experience a higher level of living.

RISK SPEAKING THE TRUTH WHEN YOUR NORMAL COURSE WOULD BE TO HESITATE

Start by taking some baby steps of faith that carry you beyond where you currently are. Ortberg says, "Begin the day by asking God for wisdom about where you need to step out of the boat and get your feet wet that day. Call someone whom you have been avoiding out of fear. Express your faith to a person who does not know about your beliefs. Take the risk of inviting someone to your church - someone you've been praying for and hoping you could get to join you. But you think, 'Nah, they'd never come!' Take the risk. Risk speaking the truth to a spouse, parent or friend when your normal course would be to hesitate.

"It does not matter whether or not all these steps turn out the way you hoped they would. Of course, things may not go the way you had envisioned them at times, but even so you are giving your faith a chance to grow."[3]   Each step of faith you take will help to widen your spiritual comfort zone. And that's a critical payoff because an expanded comfort zone leads to other payoffs in your life.

Payoff #2:
First hand exposure to a "Move of God!"

There is nothing that builds your faith quite like getting to be in on something or being there when God shows up, when He does something that just astounds you. But it's one of the payoffs of faith! God challenges us in Jeremiah 33:3, "Call to me and I will answer you and tell you great and unsearchable things you do not know."   God's saying, "I'd like to blow your mind at times with what I can do."

WHEN WE STEP OUTSIDE OUR SPIRITUAL COMFORT ZONE, WE PAVE THE WAY FOR GOD TO DO SOMETHING UNBELIEVABLE

And when we step outside our spiritual comfort zone and do something that makes us a bit uncomfortable, but we do it because we believe God wants us to, we pave the way for God to do something unbelievable. And when He does, we're never the same.

I remember when I first sensed God wanted me to take a step of faith in learning about healing prayer and taking more risks in praying for sick people who needed healing. That always seemed a bit risky to me and I would say to Him, "God, if I pray for healing and it doesn't happen, then people will be disappointed. I don't want to be a part of getting people's hopes up by praying for healing and then see them get disappointed when it doesn't happen."

God spoke to my heart one day and said, "Cal, you just pray for people and let Me worry about what I do in their lives."   So I started to pray more faithfully, fervently and specifically for people. In a lot of cases, I couldn't tell that my prayers made any difference. But I was challenged to pray for 50 people before I evaluated anything, with the whole idea being that if even one or two of those people received healing, that would keep me motivated to pray.

I will never forget the first time God moved. A lady named Doris was in the hospital with a bleeding problem the doctors couldn't figure out. I laid hands on her and prayed for God to release His healing power in her life, to touch her and stop the bleeding. Though I had a sense of God's gentle presence in that hospital room, I had no assurance that anything had happened in response to my prayer.

YOU CAN NEVER

BE A PART OF A

MOVE OF GOD AND

REMAIN THE SAME

Two days later, when I walked back into her room, I encountered a totally transformed Doris. I asked her, "How are you doing?"

She said, "Praise the Lord! I'm healed and I'm going home."

Somewhat dumbfounded, I said, "Doris, what do you mean?" (It's always hard to believe when God moves.)

She replied, "From the moment we prayed the other day, the bleeding stopped. My tests have come back clean and the doctors say I'm well!"

As far as I know, she's still well today and would likely tell you, "It's so great to be a part of a move of God." In fact, you can never be a part of a move of God and remain the same. That kind of payoff just boosts you to a whole new level of motivation in your faith.

So where are you asking God to move? Maybe you're waiting for a move in the life of someone, a move in your marriage, a move in your finances, a move in your career, or a move in your physical health. One of the payoffs is that as you continue to step out and trust God in whatever He asks you to do, you will at times experience "moves of God" that will astound you.

Doug Coe, who has a ministry in Washington D. C. that mostly involves people in politics, became acquainted with Bob, an insurance salesman who was completely unconnected with any government circles. Bob became a Christian and began to meet with Doug to learn about his faith. One day, Bob came in all excited about a statement in the Bible where Jesus says, "Ask whatever you will in My name, and you will receive it."

"Is that really true?" Bob demanded.

Doug explained, "Well, it's not a blank check. You have to take it in context of the teachings of the whole Bible on prayer. But yes - it really is true. Jesus really does answer prayer."

BOB SAW $500

SUDDENLY SPROUT

WINGS AND FLY AWAY

"Great!" Bob said. "Then I gotta start praying for something. I think I'll pray for Africa."

"That's kind of a broad target. Why don't you narrow it down to one country?" Doug advised.

"All right, I'll pray for Kenya."

"Do you know anyone in Kenya?" Doug asked.

"No."

"Ever been to Kenya?"

"No." Bob just wanted to pray for Kenya.

So Doug made an unusual arrangement with Bob. He said, "Bob, if you'll pray every day for the next six months for Kenya, and nothing extraordinary happens, I'll pay you $500. But if something remarkable happens, then you'll pay me $500. And if you don't pray every day, then the whole deal is off." It was a pretty unusual prayer program, but then Doug is a creative guy.

Bob began to pray and for a long time nothing happened. Then one night he was at a dinner in Washington. The people around the table were explaining what they did for a living when one woman said she helped run an orphanage in Kenya - the largest of its kind in her country.

Bob saw $500 suddenly sprout wings and fly away, but he was all over the conversation. He hadn't said much up to this point, but now he roared to life and pounded her with question after question.

The woman finally said to him, "You're obviously very interested in my country. You've been to Kenya before?"

"No."

"You know someone in Kenya?"

"No."

"Then how do you happen to be so curious?"

"Well, someone is kind of paying me $500 to pray . . ."

She asked Bob if he would like to come and visit Kenya and tour the orphanage. Bob was so eager to go he would have hopped a flight that night if he could have.

When Bob arrived in Kenya, he was appalled by the poverty and lack of basic health care. Upon returning to Washington, he just knew he had to do something. He began to write to large pharmaceutical companies, describing to them the vast need he had seen. He reminded them that every year they would throw away large amounts of medical supplies that went unsold. "Why not send them to this place in Kenya?" he asked. And some of them did.

GOD HAS SOMETHING UNIQUE FOR YOU. HE WANTS TO PRODUCE A FIRSTHAND "MOVE" IN YOUR LIFE.

In fact, the orphanage received more than a million dollars' worth of medical supplies. The woman telephoned Bob and said, "This is amazing! We've had the most phenomenal gifts because of letters you wrote. We would like to fly you back over and have a big party. Will you come?"

So Bob flew back to Kenya. While he was there, the president of Kenya came to the celebration, because it was the largest orphanage in the country, and offered to take Bob on a tour of Nairobi, the capital city. In the course of the tour, they saw a prison. Bob asked about a group of prisoners there.

"They're political prisoners," he was told.

"That's a bad idea," Bob said candidly. "You should let them out."

Bob finished the tour and flew back home. Sometime later, Bob received a phone call from the State Department of the United States government:

" Is this Bob?"

"Yes."

"Were you recently in Kenya?"

"Yes."

"Did you make any statements to the president about political prisoners?"

"Yes."

"What did you say?"

"I told him he should let them out."

The State Department official explained that the department had been working for years to get the release of these prisoners, but to no avail. Normal diplomatic channels and political maneuverings had led to a dead end. But now the prisoners had been released, and the State Department was told it was largely because of . . . Bob. So the government was calling to say "thanks." Unbelievable . . . but God wasn't done yet!

Several months later, the president of Kenya made a phone call to Bob. He was going to rearrange his government and select a new cabinet. Would Bob be willing to fly over and pray for him for three days while he worked on this very important task? So Bob, who was not politically connected at all, boarded a plane once more and flew back to Kenya, where he prayed and asked God for wisdom upon the leader of the nation as he selected his government. And all of this happened because one person decided to take God at His word and began praying in faith.[4]

FOCUS ON TAKING THE STEPS OF FAITH GOD WANTS YOU TO TAKE, AND YOUR LIFE WILL MAKE AN IMPACT ON OTHERS. IT'S INEVITABLE

Friend, I don't mean in any way to suggest that if you take some steps of faith that what happened to Bob will happen to you! But that's because God has something unique for you. He wants to produce a firsthand "move" in your life, not just impress you with Bob's. So what do you care so much about that you'll take the Bob Challenge and spend six months praying about it? I'm fairly confident that you'll experience a "move" of God in your life and when you do, please write and tell me the story.

Payoff #3:
The impact of your life on others!

There is nothing like being used by God to make a difference in other people's lives. And you were designed to make that difference. The question is, what do you want the legacy of your life to be?

I read about a guy named Lam Saiwing, a jeweler from China, who said that from the time he was a little boy, he had dreamed of having enough wealth to build gold toilets. Now he's gone all the way and built a gold bathroom.

The toilet bowls, wash basins, toilet brushes, toilet paper holders, mirror frames, wall-mounted chandeliers and even the wall tiles and doors are made of solid gold. The ceiling is decorated with ruby, sapphire, emerald and amber. For the privilege of using the $4.9 million ornate bathroom, customers must remove their shoes to avoid scuffing the gold tiles (makes you wonder if they dare sit down on the gold seats) and spend $138 on Lam's jewelry. Peeks at the gold commode used to be free, but now cost $14.

Now does that all sound a bit goofy? Some of us may not be building gold bathrooms, but we're living for our gold nonetheless. We've misunderstood that true success, as measured by God one day, is not going to be the amount of gold we stockpiled, but the impact we've made on others' lives. And what's the key to that impact? You focus on taking the steps of faith God wants you to take and your life will make an impact on others. It's inevitable. In fact, the Bible says you can't even give someone a drink of water in Jesus' name without it impacting a life.[5]

THE ULTIMATE GOAL OF OUR FAITH IS TO BE REWARDED WITH THE GOLD MEDAL OF ETERNAL LIFE

Imagine what it's going to feel like one day in heaven when one of your friends says, "I'm here because of you!" That's the success that no amount of gold can replace. And the beautiful thing is, when you cease to make gold watches and gold bathrooms your focus here, you'll get in on the gold that really counts.

Payoff #4:
The "award" stand in Heaven!

Our faith may bring us many wonderful experiences with God in this life. There will be answers to prayer, incredible breakthroughs, and moves of God in our lives. But the ultimate goal of our faith is to be rewarded with the gold medal of eternal life one day. That's our goal! I Peter 1:9 says, ". . . for you are receiving the goal of your faith, the salvation of your souls." Yes, we live by faith and exercise faith in God right now as we face life. And sometimes there are immediate payoffs.

But our ultimate goal is to make it home to heaven one day and to take our place on that award stand and have God Himself say, "Well done!" And then to get to spend an eternity with Him - that's amazing! I don't know what success you're chasing, but there is no success in this life that compares with spending an eternity in heaven.

THE ONLY THING THAT WILL DETERMINE WHERE WE SPEND ETERNITY IS IF WE HAVE PLACED OUR FAITH IN JESUS CHRIST

Tiger Woods has enjoyed unparalleled success as a golfer. But when asked not long ago what he would want to ask Bobby Jones, the deceased golf legend, if he could talk to him, Tiger said, "I just want to know how you make it back? If I have to leave here, how do I make it back?" His answer portrayed a deep interest in the afterlife, but also a deep ignorance of what the Bible says about it.

When we die, we don't get recycled and sent back. No, the Bible says in Hebrews 9:27, ". . . man is destined to die once and after that to face judgment." And at the judgment, the only thing that will determine where we spend eternity is if we have placed our faith in Jesus Christ. What did you do with Jesus? The decision to trust Him is the only decision that assures us the gold medal of eternal life one day in heaven.

So, I want to challenge you to cross that line of faith if you haven't done so already. You may ask, "Well how do I do that? What do I have to do to get that gold medal?"

A year ago, a man who was going through a tough season in his life stopped by my office to talk. He had been fired from his job quite unexpectedly just two weeks earlier. A bright, gifted guy, he'd been very successful in his business life, had a great wife and family, and no fears about finding the next job. But he said, "Cal, I've changed jobs before and feel like the answer is 'find another job.' But for some reason, I can't shake this one."

As we talked about success and what comprises success, I asked him how he was doing in his spiritual life. He confided in me that he knew he had never stepped across the line of faith and surrendered his heart to Jesus Christ. I shared with him that God wanted him to be sure that he was going to make the award stand in heaven one day.

God doesn't want any of us to have any question about that at all. It's not something that you just roll the dice and hope happens when you die. You can know before you die, that you are on your way to heaven and that you're going to get the gold medal of eternal life. God wants you to live with that assurance.[6] The only catch is, in order to win the gold, you have to be a perfect ten!

ONLY GOD

CAN CLAIM

ABSOLUTE

PERFECTION

The problem is, the Bible tells us in Romans 3:23 that "all of us have sinned and fallen short of the glory of God." Only God can claim absolute perfection. I haven't met anyone, no matter how moral or good they were, who would honestly say that they were perfect.

So if it takes a ten to win the gold medal of eternal life, and none of us can claim a ten, then we all fall short, right? Which leads to another question: "If all of us are something less than ten, where's God's cutoff point?" If I'm a five, I sure hope he'll let fives in. If you're a four, you hope fours get in. Sevens hope sevens get in, etc.

Some people say, "God doesn't have a cutoff point. He'll just forgive everybody." Really? You mean to tell me Osama Bin Laden can go around blowing people up and God will just forgive him? A person can serve Satan and evil all his life and it makes no difference? Come on! A holy God distinguishes between good and evil. The only problem is, He's so holy that only a ten will do!

That's the bad news. None of us can score high enough on our own to make it to heaven. All of our exercises to impress God with our score are futile, even if we manage a 9.9. It's still not a ten. But here's the great news. God loved you so much and wanted to give you the gold medal of eternal life so much that He devised a way for you to score a perfect ten. His answer to that dilemma was the person of Jesus Christ.

IF ALL OF US ARE SOMETHING LESS THAN 10, WHERE'S GOD'S CUTOFF POINT?

When Jesus Christ died on the cross, He wasn't dying for His sins. The Bible says He was without sin.[7] He was a perfect ten. Now Jesus says to each of us, "If you will accept Me as your substitute, as the person who stood in for your sin, and if you'll surrender your life to Me, no matter what the score, and by faith trust what I have done for you, I will take your sub-ten score and nail it to the cross. At the same time, I will place my ten on you and my ten will get you into heaven!"

2 Corinthians 5:21 says: "God made Him who had no sin (*Jesus: the perfect ten*) to be sin for us (*the sub-tens*), so that in Him we might become the righteousness of God (*we become perfect tens*)." There's the great exchange. God says, "Look, you need a ten, but you can't provide it yourself. Because I loved you so much, I provided a ten for you! Now if you'll surrender your life to Jesus, in union with Him, your imperfect score will be nailed to the cross, and His perfect score will become yours."

That great exchange happens through an act of faith whereby you say, "I'm committing my life and staking my eternity on what Jesus did for me, and from now on, I'm going to follow Him by faith."

When my friend understood that, he did what I hope you will do, if you haven't done so already. He surrendered his life to Jesus, by faith. And in that moment, he secured the greatest success anyone can ever experience in this life. At that moment of faith, his name was entered into the book of life in heaven, which guarantees his place on the ultimate victory stand one day.

I want to challenge you to make a decision right now that you are going to live your life by faith. You are going to live at a higher level because your goal, from this day forward, is going to be following Jesus by faith, until that day when you make it home. If you have never personally trusted Jesus, I want to challenge you to take that step today and, by an act of faith, invite Jesus Christ to come into your life.

WHEN JESUS CHRIST

DIED ON THE CROSS,

HE WASN'T DYING

FOR HIS SINS

If it's your desire to begin a faith walk with Jesus today, and you know you've never invited Him into your heart, then I want you to pray this prayer right now:

Lord Jesus, today I want to begin a faith journey with you. By faith, right now, I believe that you are who you said you were, the only Son of God. By faith, I believe you, a perfect ten, died on the cross in my place to pay the penalty for my sins. I admit that I'm something far less than a perfect ten. Please forgive me and cancel out all my sins today. By faith, I believe you rose from the grave, proving yourself to be the Lord of Life. And because of that, you are able to give life to me. I now invite you to enter my life and to give me fullness and purpose right now, and eternal life when this one is over. Fill me with your Holy Spirit and direct my life from this day forward. As you teach me and lead me, it's my desire to obey whatever you tell me to do. Thank you Lord, that today, I have begun a whole new life that will never end! In Jesus Name, Amen."

YOU ARE GOING TO LIVE AT A HIGHER LEVEL BECAUSE YOUR GOAL, FROM THIS DAY FORWARD, IS GOING TO BE FOLLOWING JESUS BY FAITH, UNTIL THAT DAY WHEN YOU MAKE IT HOME

Now friend, if you prayed that prayer and sincerely placed your trust in Jesus today, you have begun a whole new life. Your sins have been forgiven. You have become a new creation. God has given you eternal life! Heaven is going to be your home because you trusted Jesus. I'm delighted that you began a life of faith today. From now, until the day you meet Jesus, may you pursue living at a higher level of faith.

NOTES

Chapter 1: Understanding the Importance of Faith

1. Jim Cymbala, *Fresh Faith* (Grand Rapids: Zondervan Publishing, 1999), 192.
2. "Frugal Woman Leaves $3.5 Million to WKU" *Courier Journal of Louisville,* 27, September, 2001
3. John 3:16; Acts 2:21; Ephesians 1:7; Colossians 1:13,14
4. Jim Cymbala, *Fresh Faith* (Grand Rapids: Zondervan Publishing, 1999), 201.

Chapter 2: Releasing Faith's Potential

1. Max Lucado, *The Applause of Heaven* (Dallas: Word Publishing, 1990), 39.
2. Wayne Cordeiro, *Doing Church as a Team* (Ventura,CA: Regal Books, 2001) 128-29.

Chapter 3: Laying a Sure Foundation For Faith

1. Tim Hansel, *Holy Sweat* (Waco: Word Publishing, 1987), 46-47.
2. Jeffrey L. Sheler, "Is the Bible True," *U.S. News &World Report,* 25 October, 1999, 52.
3. Ibid., 50-59.

Chapter 4: Developing a Deeper Faith

1. Max Lucado, *He Chose the Nails* (Dallas: Word Publishing, 2000), 45-46.

Chapter 5: Overcoming Obstacles to Faith

1. Eleanor Wright, *Naaman,* Songs of Promise-BMI, 1984
2. Acts 10:34.
3. Eleanor Wright, *Naaman,* Songs of Promise-BMI, 1984

Chapter 6: Facing the Risk-Factor In Faith

1. Karl Taro Greenfeld, "Life On the Edge," *Time,* 6 September, 1999, 31.
2. Ibid., 31.
3. Ibid., 32.

4. Ibid., 36.
5. Larry Laudin, quoted in John Ortberg, *If You Want To Walk On The Water, You've Got To Get Out of The Boat* (Grand Rapids: Zondervan Publishing, 2001), 20.
6. Eileen Guder, quoted in Bill and Kathy Peel, *Discover Your Destiny* (Colorado Springs: Nav Press, 1996), 25.
7. Ann Landers, *The Dilemma*
8. Charles Murray, quoted in John Maxwell, *Be All You Can Be* (Wheaton, Victor Books, 1987) 169.
9. John Maxwell, *Develop The Leader Within You* (Nashville: Nelson Publishers, 1993), 166.

Chapter 7: Building A Tenacious Faith
1. Rick Warren, *How To Keep On Believing,* audiotape from a sermon at Saddleback Community Church, 1 Saddleback Parkway, Lake Forest, CA 92630 on 25, 26 November, 2000.

Chapter 9: Leaving a Legacy of Faith
1. Rick Reilly, "Welcome To the Real World," *Sports Illustrated,* 19 August, 2002
2. Bruce Wilkinson, *First Hand Faith* (Gresham, OR: Vision House Publishing, 1996), 9-10.

Chapter 10: Enjoying Faith's Payoff
1. John Ortberg, *If You Want To Walk On The Water, You've Got To Get Out of The Boat* (Grand Rapids: Zondervan Publishing, 2001), 83.
2. Ibid., 83.
3. Ibid., 83.
4. Ibid., 91-93.
5. Matthew 10:42; Mark 9:41
6. I John 5:13
7. Hebrews 4:15